AFGHANISTAN

lifting the veil

ISBN 0-13-047951-9

90000

9 780130 479518

AFGHANISTAN
lifting the veil

REUTERS

Published by **Prentice Hall**

Library of Congress Cataloging-in-Publication Data

A CIP catalog record for this book can be obtained from the Library of Congress

Publisher: Tim Moore
Executive editor: Jim Boyd
Director of production: Sophie Papanikolaou
Production supervisor: Patti Guerrieri
Marketing manager: Bryan Gambrel
Manufacturing manager: Maura Zaldivar
Editorial assistant: Allyson Kloss
Cover design director: Jerry Votta
Cover designer: Anthony Gemmellaro
Art director: Gail Cocker-Bogusz
Interior design and layout: Meg Van Arsdale

Reuters: Stephen Jukes
Front and back cover art photographer: Yannis Behrakis
Cover photo copyright © 2001 Reuters
Foreword copyright © 2002 Sebastian Junger

In compiling this book, thanks go to many people. At Reuters: Andrew Browne, Adam Cox, Steve Crisp, Mikhail Evstafiev, Anton Ferreira, Izabel Grindal, Sonya Hepinstall, Gary Hershorn, Chaitanya Kalbag, Jane Macartney, Peter Millership, Paul Mylrea, Alexia Singh, Tom Szlukovenyi, Irina Stocker, and David Viggers.

© 2002 Reuters
Published by Prentice Hall PTR
A division of Pearson Education, Inc.
Upper Saddle River, NJ 07458

Prentice Hall books are widely used by corporations and government agencies
for training, marketing, and resale.

The publisher offers discounts on this book when ordered in bulk quantities.
For more information, contact: Corporate Sales Department, Phone: 800-382-3419;
Fax: 201-236-7141; E-mail: corpsales@prenhall.com; or write: Prentice Hall PTR,
Corp. Sales Dept., One Lake Street, Upper Saddle River, NJ 07458.

Printed in the United States of America

10 9 8 7 6 5 4 3 2 1

ISBN 0-13-047951-9

Pearson Education LTD.
Pearson Education Australia PTY, Limited
Pearson Education Singapore, Pte. Ltd.
Pearson Education North Asia Ltd.
Pearson Education Canada, Ltd.
Pearson Educación de Mexico, S.A. de C.V.
Pearson Education—Japan
Pearson Education Malaysia, Pte. Ltd.

We dedicate this book to our Reuters colleagues,

Harry Burton and *Azizullah Haidari*,

who were killed in an ambush in
Afghanistan on November 19, 2001.

Contents

Foreword

We got the terrible news around noon. We were crouched in the dust with several hundred Northern Alliance troops, waiting for the order to attack, when we got word that three journalists had just been killed up north outside Taloqan. Two men and a woman had been captured and executed by Taliban fighters, we'd heard, after they fell off an armored personnel carrier during a battle.

The details were wrong—in fact they'd been shot in an ambush—but the implications were the same: The Taliban were targeting journalists.

I was at a position called Du Saraka, half a mile from the Taliban lines, and the final attack on Kabul was supposed to happen in less than an hour. I sat glumly in the seat of our pickup truck, listening to outgoing artillery rip over our heads. Any number of grim scenarios could unfold now, including—and this I found to be the most horrifying—the Northern Alliance could get lured into a massive trap and then be wiped out. If we went forward with them, we would be captured, and the Taliban had just issued an edict that all foreign reporters would be executed as spies. Maybe that was what was awaiting us; none of us knew. I took my notebook and wrote: "We're supposed to attack in half an hour. I can't believe how much I don't want to do this."

One television crew decided to pull out; they came up to us one by one to say goodbye. They told us to be careful, and they walked away shaking their heads. It got worse. A news agency reporter came walking back into camp with a sniper round in the middle of his back. It had knocked him down. The steel plate in his flak jacket had stopped it. Not long after that, a radio call came in to one of the commanders, and the Northern Alliance tanks rattled to life, belching yellow smoke. This was it.

Every war reporter returns home to the inevitable question: Is it really worth it? Is covering someone else's war really worth jeopardizing the wonderful life that you have? It's a strangely condescending question, as if the speakers think they're raising an issue that we journalists, in our blazing idealism and ambition, are incapable of raising on our own. Ironically, by then it's a very easy question to answer—of course it was worth it. We returned safely, didn't we? The decision to follow this attack or drive that particular stretch of road was demonstrably a good one, and now here we are at a cocktail party telling our stories.

But what we wouldn't give for that knowledge when we need it. Every journalist in Afghanistan has agonized over the decision of whether to proceed forward, and since there are no easy answers, no firm guarantees, we resort to a strangely passive fatalism. In the end, danger is never where you think it is, and second-guessing every single decision becomes so agonizing in its own right, that it's easier to just shrug and see what happens.

The doubt is eased only slightly by the belief, naïve or otherwise, that what we are doing is actually important. Nowhere was that more true than in Afghanistan, where the journalists understood that they were watching not just a war but a turning point in history. September 11 changed everything, we realized, and we were in one of the most remote countries of the world to watch its immediate aftermath. As a journalist—as a human being—I felt it an honor, even a duty, to be there. That slim belief formed the basis of whatever resolve I was able to muster while waiting there unhappily in the dust to attack.

Eight foreign journalists were killed during the week that Kabul fell—three in the ambush outside Taloqan, four on the road between Kabul and Jalalabad, and one during a late-night robbery in Mazar-i-Sharif. By contrast, only one American soldier was killed, a statistic that says much about the changing role of journalists—not to mention American soldiers—in modern war.

Why was Afghanistan so deadly? First there was the famous Afghan hospitality which, as applied to journalists, meant that we could go absolutely anywhere and do anything we wanted. We were free to get ourselves killed, in other words, and for journalists accustomed to the bureaucratic roadblocks of Bosnia and the Gulf War, such liberties were almost disorienting.

To make matters worse, the war had dragged on for a full month with almost no ground movement at all, so by the time things started to happen, journalists were beside themselves with impatience. Thousands had been stuck in Pakistan, unable to cross the border, and thousands more were arrayed across Northern Afghanistan, living in mud houses and surviving on rice and mutton. When the ground war finally started, it was such a relief—and the Taliban offered so little resistance—that at times it seemed more like a staged media event than a real war.

It got real very quickly. The three journalists were shot off an APC in Taloqan, then four were stopped on the road outside Kabul and executed. Two of them—Azizullah Haidari and Harry Burton—were Reuters correspondents. News of their deaths came to us in Kabul, while we were celebrating the fall of Kabul and wondering why the war had ended so quickly. It was another dose of reality in a country that even experienced journalists kept misjudging. It's very easy to fall prey to the misconception that front lines are the most dangerous place in a war; in fact, they're so creepy and terrifying that you act with an embarrassing amount of caution.

What is much harder to do is perceive the threat in an otherwise peaceful situation. The only time I have truly been in danger—in Sierra Leone, a country not unlike Afghanistan in its chaos and volatility—I was nowhere near a front line. I was driving a supposedly safe road outside Freetown, and I was stopped by a group of rebels called the Westside Boys. A lot of guns got cocked before it was over, and I felt extremely lucky to get out of there alive.

Haidari and Burton died in a similar situation. I know many journalists who feed off the intensity of front-line reporting, but I'm afraid we're all cowards when it comes to the idea of roadside execution. I have tried—and failed—to conjure in my mind the horror and desolation of those last few minutes; I think every journalist in Kabul must have tried to imagine it. With one exception, theirs were the last deaths in Afghanistan. They died in a manner that was so chilling, cold-blooded, and unnecessary that it may well have brought the unbelievably high death toll of journalists to a halt. It made us realize that this was for real, that a mistake meant we weren't going home.

After a decade of reporting, I'm still amazed by how easy that is to forget.

Sebastian Junger
February 2002

In Memoriam

Azizullah Haidari and Harry Burton were both 33 years old when they died on November 19, 2001. They had grown up thousands of miles apart, Aziz as an Afghan refugee in Pakistan, Harry in a more secure Australia. But they had much in common. Both trained for other vocations—Aziz as a teacher, Harry as an agriculturalist—and were drawn to journalism by a common curiosity and a thirst to share their discoveries with the rest of the world. Both grew up in large families. Both inspired their friends and colleagues with their energy, enthusiasm, and commitment.

And both of them started out in excitement and anticipation that Monday in November on the highway from Jalalabad to Kabul, in a convoy with other journalists. They were eager to gather the latest news on the U.S.-led campaign in Afghanistan. Nobody will know with certainty what happened that day on the dusty shoulder of an Afghan highway, but Aziz and Harry and two other journalists—Maria Grazia Cutuli and Julio Fuentes—were tragically cut down in an ambush by armed men.

Their deaths, and those of four other journalists in Afghanistan in the winter of 2001, struck cruel blows against the quest to report the news truthfully and fairly. The courage of the men and women reporting the news is robust and resilient. They are appalled by such killings but pick themselves up quickly.

This book is a collection of the best pictures that Reuters photographers have shot in Afghanistan and of vivid words from some of the writers who have chronicled the tortured nation's history for more than two decades.

It is dedicated to Aziz and Harry from their Reuters colleagues, who unite in saying: "We will remember them."

Chaitanya Kalbag
Editor, Reuters Asia Pacific

AFGHANISTAN

lifting the veil

The Tormented State

Tom Heneghan

Montstuart Elphinstone, the first British envoy to what he called the "Kingdom of Caubul," tried to convince a tribal elder in 1809 that the Pashtuns would do better living peacefully under an absolute monarch. The old man replied: "We are content with discord, we are content with alarms, we are content with blood, but we will never be content with a master."

The clouds of dust from the collapsed World Trade Center had hardly settled before the search for culprits focused on an impoverished country half a world away—Afghanistan. Osama bin Laden, prime suspect in the devastating attack on the United States, was based there in a network of caves and mud-walled forts in mountain hideouts so remote that only four-by-fours, hikers, or donkeys could reach them. Within weeks, U.S. bombers were blasting strongholds of the country's Taliban rulers who had given bin Laden shelter and refused to give him up. American special forces and CIA operatives donned dust scarves and flat pakol caps to take up arms alongside local anti-Taliban fighters. Television viewers were bombarded with images of the black-turbaned Taliban, the long blue burqas their women had to wear, and young boys reciting the Koran at madrassa mosque schools that spread Islamic radicalism.

How did it happen that Afghanistan, with its reputation as a graveyard for invaders dating from the nineteenth century, became a safe haven for bin Laden and his al Qaeda network? How did the country that was once a haunt of Western hippies seeking peace, love, and happiness earn a new reputation as the lair of the world's most-wanted man?

First look at the landscape. This is a country of snow-topped mountain ranges, steep rocky valleys, and endless rows of barren hills. Cities are few and far between. Apart from the battered cars and patchy electricity supply, many towns and villages look unchanged from centuries ago. The traveler's eye focuses on the country's breathtaking natural beauty. The military eye sees terrain easy to defend and almost impossible to conquer.

Next study a map. Afghanistan lies at the western end of the massive mountain chain that rings the northern rim of the Indian subcontinent. Two main land routes lead to the fertile plains of India, one from the ancient empire of Persia, the other through the later major power Russia. Some of the passes and valleys also formed part of the fabled Silk Road between the Middle East and China. These trade and invasion routes all run through Afghanistan, making geography the main determinant of the country's destiny.

Now meet the people. Dozens of ethnic groups live here on the fringes of the modern world. Afghans offer unbounded hospitality to guests and ruthless violence to enemies. There are Pashtuns, Tajiks, Hazaras, Uzbeks, Turkomans, Aimaqs, Nuristanis—the list goes on and on. It sounds like a recipe for ethnic strife ready to explode into a Yugoslav-style breakup, but the rivalry has never raged that far. Centuries of fighting off foreign invaders have forged a keen sense of a common Afghan identity.

Finally, attend a traditional buzkashi game. This wild contest pits a horseman holding a headless goat against dozens of other riders trying to steal it from him. Fast, brutal, and sometimes even deadly, this free-for-all is a microcosm of Afghan politics itself. There are no rules, no teams, and no partners. Scoring is often secondary to simply playing the game.

From Invasions to the Great Game

Afghanistan has tried almost every form of government except Western-style democracy without ever creating a stable state. For much of its history the country had such uncertain boundaries and rulers that it did not even have an official name. The Pashtuns, the core of its ethnic kaleidoscope, lived in an unruly confederation of tribes that fought each other when they were not at war with outside powers. Montstuart Elphinstone, the first British envoy to what he called the "Kingdom of Caubul," tried to convince a tribal elder in 1809 that the Pashtuns would do better living peacefully under an absolute monarch. The old man replied: "We are content with discord, we are content with alarms, we are content with blood, but we will never be content with a master."

Survival rather than statecraft has long been the main concern in this region. Located at the crossroads of Central and South Asia, Afghanistan has been a battlefield since the Aryan invasions six centuries ago. Many centuries earlier fabled invaders, including Alexander the Great and Genghis Khan, had passed through and plundered. The Afghans turned the tide in the early 1500s, when Emperor Babur swept down from Kabul to Delhi to establish the famed Moghul dynasty that ruled India until Britain colonized the subcontinent.

Afghanistan took its first step into the modern age in 1747, when its Pashtun tribes elected Ahmad Shah Abdali as their king, launching the Durrani dynasty that lasted until 1973.

Afghanistan was still so isolated in 1800 that none of the great European powers of the day even had a reliable map of it. Two mighty empires, British India and Tsarist Russia, were slowly advancing their frontiers toward this black hole when Napoleon approached the Russians and Persians with plans to cross Afghanistan to invade India. Alarm bells rang in London. Britain decided to extend its control throughout western India—roughly the territory of present-day Pakistan—and deep into the Hindu Kush. Soldiers and spies would fan out through the uncharted mountains to map invasion routes, scout out local tribes, and win allies for the Crown. It was the start of what Rudyard Kipling dubbed "the Great Game" for power and influence over the mountains of Afghanistan.

This "forward policy" decreed Afghanistan should be a pro-British buffer state to keep Russia at a safe distance from India. The Army of the Indus seized Kabul in 1839 and reinstated a deposed king as its puppet. When Afghan resentment burst into violence, mobs murdered several officers and forced 4,500 British and Indian troops and 12,000 camp followers to leave Kabul in January 1842 to march to the safety of India.

Only one man, army doctor William Brydon, survived the savage ambushes in the snow-filled mountain passes to make it to Jalalabad, near the Khyber Pass, to tell the harrowing story.

Undaunted, Britain launched a second war in 1879–1880 to ward off fresh Russian approaches to Kabul. A British force again occupied the city, and the mobs again rose up and killed the unwanted foreigners. After hitting back hard and hanging ringleaders in retaliation, the occupying forces found that this time they did not even have a puppet Afghan ruler to install on the throne. Abdur Rehman, nephew of the king they had just deposed, returned from exile and was promptly offered the throne and generous aid as long as he let British India conduct all his foreign affairs. A Third Afghan War briefly broke out in 1919, when the reformist King Amanullah renounced British control over Kabul's foreign affairs. Neither side had much heart for a fight, and they quickly signed a treaty that left Afghanistan fully independent again.

Molding a Modern State

Following the second Anglo-Afghan war, the Durrani kings experimented with tyranny, with fast-forward Westernization, and with gradual reform, trying to find the best way to forge a modern state. The most consistent lesson they learned was that change in Afghanistan can only be slow, and opposition to unwanted change can be violent.

Abdur Rehman, who ruled from 1880 to 1901, used medieval methods—harsh repression, ethnic cleansing, forced resettlement, and anti-Shi'ite pogroms—to lay the foundations of the modern Afghan state. Along the way, the "Iron Amir" crushed over 40 tribal revolts against his rule. The country was carved into provinces with loyal governors, who slowly replaced tribal elders as the main local authority. But Abdur Rehman was no Westernizer. Wary of meddlers, he refused to allow railroads or even telegraph lines to cross his borders. The economy stagnated. "Much of the subsequent ethnic tensions in northern Afghanistan and the inter-ethnic massacres after 1997 can be traced back to the Iron Amir's policies," wrote Ahmed Rashid in *Taliban*, his best-selling study of the harsh Islamic movement.

Modeling himself after the Turkish reformer Kemal Ataturk, King Amanullah opted for fast-forward Westernization during his reign from 1919 to 1929. He had the country's first written constitution drawn up, established an independent judiciary, and enhanced women's rights. After a grand tour of Europe in 1927 he decreed even faster change, announcing that women would go without veils, civil servants would be limited to one wife, and everyone would have to wear Western clothes in Kabul. To press home his point, he had Queen Soraya remove her veil before a shocked assembly of notables. In the tribal revolt that followed, an illiterate Tajik bandit named Bacha Saqqao seized power and sent Amanullah rushing off to India in his brand-new Rolls Royce.

The last Durrani king, Zahir Shah, was only 19 when he assumed the throne in 1933. For the next 20 years the French-educated monarch let his uncles run the country and slowly open it more to the outside world. In the 1950s, Cold War rivalry drove Afghanistan's development agenda as the Soviet Union and the United States tried to outdo each other in offering aid. Moscow paved the capital's streets, erected municipal buildings, and built the Salang Tunnel through the Hindu Kush. Washington responded with a highway across southern Afghanistan, an international airport in Kandahar, and an ambitious irrigation project in the Helmand Valley. The leaders of both superpowers even visited the country—Soviet premier Nikita Khrushchev in 1955 and U.S. President Dwight Eisenhower in 1959. But the United States turned down several requests for military aid, after which Kabul turned to Moscow and received a wide selection of tanks, fighter jets, bombers, helicopters, and small arms.

When Zahir Shah began to exercise his powers as king, he proved to be a firm but gradual modernizer. The proof came in the 1964 constitution, the most liberal the country had ever seen. It set up a constitutional monarchy with a bicameral parliament, the lower house being elected by secret ballot and the upper house partly elected and partly appointed by the king. Although framed in an Islamic context, the legal system was secular and included equal rights for women and freedom of expression. "This was perhaps the high point of consensus between the traditional and educated sections of Afghan society, the latter urbanized, the former overwhelmingly rural," wrote Martin Ewans, a former British diplomat in Kabul. What followed was a lively decade marked by political debate and student activism. "I was a teenager then and I remember that time well, it was like a golden age," Hamid Karzai told me in late September 2001, just before the anti-Taliban campaign was launched that made him interim prime minister by the end of the year.

War and Chaos

The golden age turned red, first politically and then literally, after the bloodless coup of 1973. Mohammad Daoud, Zahir Shah's cousin, seized power while the king was vacationing in Italy. Daoud cracked down on growing Islamic unrest, prompting many future leaders of the anti-Soviet jihad (holy war), including the most famous commander, Ahmad Shah Masood, to flee to Pakistan. When he began purging Communists from the military, left-wing officers staged a bloody coup in 1978 and massacred Daoud and his family. Power passed to Nur Mohammad Taraki, a former U.S embassy translator who led a small Communist party. Taraki boldly decreed sweeping land reforms, launched mass literacy classes, and replaced the black, red, and green Afghan flag with a red banner. Once again, tribal leaders and religious figures rose up to resist. But before they could topple him, a rival Communist named Hafizullah Amin launched a coup in September 1979 in which Taraki was killed. Amin lasted only until late December. When Soviet troops invaded, he was murdered, and another Communist named Babrak Karmal came to power. The invasion prompted an international outcry, heightened East-West tensions, and unleashed a guerrilla war that would eventually bring the mighty Soviet Union to its knees.

The superpowers quickly turned this into a proxy war in which all major decisions were beyond the Afghans' control. Moscow sent in 115,000 men backed by all the firepower of the huge Soviet arsenal. The United States, China, Saudi Arabia, Egypt, Pakistan, and other states funneled billions of dollars and tons of arms to seven rebel parties based in Peshawar. As the main channel for this, Pakistan's Inter-Services Intelligence agency doled out arms and aid to commanders it favored—usually radical Islamic Pashtuns it hoped to manipulate—and withheld them from more independent parties. Soviet forces secured the main cities, where Karmal tried to push through Communist reforms, but their hold over the countryside was shaky.

During two visits in 1986, Kabul seemed to me an island of modern life in a country that was sliding backward. The government promoted mass education, public housing, and health services. Many women had shed the all-enveloping burqa veil in favor of Western-style dresses, and educated women had prominent posts in the government. While Islam was officially respected, Dutch beer and Soviet vodka were openly sold. Kabulis generally disliked the Russians, but many had little taste, either, for the rural rebels who threatened to turn back what progress the capital had achieved.

The war also shattered the Afghan economy, already one of the feeblest in the world. Gross domestic product is estimated to have fallen by half between 1980 and 1994, while prices rocketed a thousandfold. The only crop that flourished was the opium poppy, annual production of which leaped from about 200 tons in 1978 to 2,000 by 1990. Much of this was refined into heroin and exported to flood the streets of the United States and Western Europe.

Afghanistan gradually became Moscow's Vietnam. The Communists could not defeat the rebels despite frequent Soviet carpet-bombing, ground offensives, and massacres of civilians. The war was also a political disaster, since it produced the world's largest exodus of refugees—4.5 million in Pakistan and Iran. Soon after taking office in 1985, the reformist Soviet leader Mikhail Gorbachev concluded the war was not worth it and decided to pull his troops out. The last soldiers crossed the bridge over the Oxus River onto Soviet soil on February 15, 1989, sealing the most humiliating defeat for Russia since it began expanding into Central Asia in 1552.

During the war, Afghanistan became a magnet for young foreign Muslims eager to spread Islamic revolution. Between 1982 and 1992 an estimated 35,000 men from 43 Islamic countries in the Arab world, Central Asia, and the Far East earned their spurs fighting with the mujahideen or training at Islamist camps. One of them was Osama bin Laden, who used his family fortune and donations from Saudi princes and Islamic charities to support the Arab recruits. "The camps became virtual universities for future Islamic radicalism," wrote Ahmed Rashid. When Moscow withdrew, Washington hailed this as a victory for the West and walked away from the larger Afghan crisis. But Muslim extremists saw it as a triumph for Islam and began fanning out to repeat it elsewhere. Over the next few years, Islamic Jihad in the West Bank, Abu Sayyaf in the Philippines, Harakat-ul-Ansar in Kashmir, and other Muslim groups used their Afghan experience to foment unrest in their home countries. Bin Laden's mostly Arab group, al Qaeda, took aim at the United States itself, starting with the World Trade Center bombing in 1993.

When the rebels finally captured Kabul in 1992, the fractious leaders were so divided they could hardly agree on a government. The power-sharing deal they finally came up with was doomed by its own complexity. Sibghatullah Mojaddedi served as interim president for two months and handed power to Burhanuddin Rabbani, the ethnic Tajik head of the Jamiat-i-Islami party that is the core of today's Northern Alliance. Rabbani was supposed to rule for only four months, but he was hardly in office when the sidelined Pashtun firebrand Gulbuddin Hekmatyar launched furious rocket attacks on Kabul. Jamiat commander Masood fought back, while Rabbani responded by breaking their deal and having himself declared president. Cease-fires regularly collapsed into furious battles that devastated western Kabul and killed thousands of innocent residents. So, after winning a 15-year war, the mujahideen lost the peace soon after coming to power. Chaos and crime prevailed as warlords divided the country into their personal fiefdoms.

Omar and Osama

With all central authority gone, a movement called the Taliban—"religious students"—moved in to restore law and order. Starting in 1994, they swept through the Pashtun belt, deposing corrupt local warlords and imposing their harsh version of Islam. They first seemed interested just in restoring law and order, and residents welcomed them. But a wider potential soon became apparent to neighboring Pakistan. The government, military, and traders were keen to secure the roads leading to the markets of the newly independent Central Asian republics. If Afghanistan were pacified, oil and gas pipelines could be built across its territory to bring energy from Central Asia to Pakistan and the world market. A U.S. oil company, UNOCAL, showed a keen interest, and Washington was initially positive. With not very covert support from the Pakistani military, the young fighters, mostly recruited from refugee camps in Pakistan, quickly seized Kandahar, Afghanistan's second-largest city, and other points along the main highway running through the south and west.

Their leaders, who finally seized Kabul in 1996, imposed the strictest Islamic regime ever seen. Women were banned from work and girls from school, men were ordered to grow long beards, television was stopped, TV sets were smashed and cinemas closed, while even innocent fun like kite flying was banned. Contemptuous of Afghanistan's pre-Islamic past, they destroyed the huge Buddha statues carved into the hillside at Bamiyan and smashed Kabul Museum's famous collection of ancient Buddhist-Greek statues. Power shifted to Kandahar, eclipsing Kabul and the central government bureaucracy. Essential services like health were often left to foreign aid groups to provide, and then those groups were harassed to the point that foreign staff had to leave.

One exception to its puritanism was the blind eye the Taliban turned on opium production. Output more than doubled under the Taliban to 4,581 tons in 1999, making Afghanistan the world's biggest producer. But in 2000 they banned opium cultivation altogether—probably their only policy decision applauded abroad.

With its weak state and radical Islamic ideology, the Taliban's Afghanistan was an ideal location for bin Laden. He had already used his family fortune to help build a tunnel complex in the mountains around Khost, near the Pakistani border, as an arms dump, training ground, and medical center for the mujahideen. In 1989 he set up al Qaeda ("the base") in Peshawar as an office to help Arabs training or fighting in Afghanistan. After moving from country to country several times in the early 1990s, he returned to Afghanistan in 1996, arriving by charter jet in Jalalabad with his three wives, 13 children, and dozens of Arab militants.

At bin Laden's original cave network near Khost in February 1998, al Qaeda called for a jihad against "Jews and Crusaders." A fatwa (religious edict) it issued stated: "The ruling to kill the Americans and their allies—civilians and military—is an individual duty for every Muslim who can do it in any country in which it is possible to." When extremists followed the call that August and bombed the U.S. embassies in Kenya and Tanzania, killing 220 people, Washington hit back by unleashing 70 cruise missiles against the camps around Khost and Jalalabad.

Al Qaeda gradually became a state within a state in Afghanistan. Bin Laden supplied Mullah Omar with hundreds of Arab fighters to help in his campaigns against Ahmad Shah Masood, who still defended a corner of northeastern Afghanistan against the Taliban steamroller. The Taliban forces were mostly local tribal militias and scattered units of trained soldiers and officers, while the al Qaeda forces were better trained and equipped and fiercer in battle. As pressure on the Taliban grew, Mullah Omar

came to rely increasingly on al Qaeda. They were ready to fight to the death, unlike many of their Afghan comrades-in-arms. How closely the two movements worked together became evident on September 9, 2001, when two Arab suicide bombers posing as journalists killed Masood during a purported interview. Two days later, the pattern became clear. Bin Laden had eliminated the best potential ally for the United States in any campaign to retaliate for the attacks on the World Trade Center and the Pentagon.

A Subdued New Dawn

When the U.S. bombing campaign helped topple the Taliban in November 2001, Afghanistan again found itself at the end of a war but not at the end of its troubles. Not a single politician at home or abroad could claim enough support to become the next national leader. All the known names had tried and failed to govern in the 1990s. Many had fought ferocious battles against each other in the bloody civil war. The nominal president Burhanuddin Rabbani, head of the Northern Alliance, was a discredited and controversial figure after his disastrous four years as head of state in the 1990s. Other former mujahideen party leaders were political has-beens. One dark horse with some support in Washington was former mujahideen commander Abdul Haq. But the Taliban executed him in late October when they caught him trying to rally tribes in eastern Afghanistan against them. It was testimony to the complete lack of leadership Afghanistan faced that many Afghans looked to 87-year-old exiled king Zahir Shah as their savior. Zahir Shah had been living in Rome for 28 years and played no role during the long years of war. To expect this frail man to lead the unprecedented reconstruction was a leap of faith even for such fervent believers as the Afghans.

But a younger generation of Afghans, the second tier of leaders behind the long-time party chiefs, was determined to make hope triumph over experience. These were men in their 40s who had been fighting since they were teenagers. The most prominent were the new "triumvirate" in the Northern Alliance who vowed to set up the broad-based democracy they said their slain master Masood had wanted. So the three—Interior Minister Yunis Qanuni, Foreign Minister Abdullah Abdullah, and Defense Minister Mohammad Fahim—announced the decidedly un-Afghan line that they would share power in a post-Taliban government. Their Pashtun rivals were deeply suspicious, and even more so when the Alliance marched into Kabul on November 13 despite appeals from abroad not to occupy the capital. But politics had lagged far behind the progress of the war, which chased out the Taliban so quickly that no time was left to agree in advance on an all-party government.

In late November the Northern Alliance met with three exile Afghan groups in Bonn for talks on this transitional government. Mindful of their earlier failures, the United Nations hosts bluntly warned the groups not to lose the peace again. But the delegates needed no lessons. They knew how disastrous failure would be this time. The Afghan people were sick and tired of war, and the international community knew it had to help create stability in Afghanistan if it wanted to stamp out extremism there. After eight days of almost round-the-clock negotiations, they agreed on an interim administration for six months, followed by a traditional Loya Jirga, or grand council, to name a transitional leadership for the next 18 months. Then, after two years of appointed leadership Afghanistan would hold free elections for a democratic parliament.

Their choice for interim prime minister, Hamid Karzai, was a bridge between traditional and modern Afghanistan. Karzai was chief of the large Popalzai tribe from the Kandahar area and scion of a royalist family with a tradition of public service. Already a Pashtun elder at the age of 43, he could reassure traditionalists in the east and south who were steadfastly opposed to seeing a Tajik or other northern minority leader in Kabul. Hardly known to most Afghans, he proved his anti-Taliban credentials by slipping into the country in early October to rally tribes against the fundamentalists and helping to negotiate the Taliban departure from Kandahar. At the same time, he had a string of modern skills, including fluent English honed as a student in India and a frequent visitor to the United States. Here was a Pashtun from the south who could work with the triumvirate from the north.

At his swearing in on December 22, Karzai made an eloquent appeal for peace and vowed to rebuild the nation, protect freedom of speech and religion, and respect women's rights. "Today we are happy that we can see the sun rising again on our land," he declared. "I think a wave of peace and unity is coming to our country."

But even at this new dawn, he could not avoid recalling how often his country's hopes had been dashed in the past. "If we deliver to the Afghan people what we promised, this will be a great day," he said after his inauguration. "If we don't deliver, this will go into oblivion."

Soldiers fighting for the opposition Northern Alliance pray on the front line at the border of Kunduz province, the only province in northern Afghanistan which was still under control of the crumbling Taliban forces, November 22, 2001. The besieged province would fall within days. In the background is a Soviet-era tank.

Gleb Garanich

A Northern Alliance fighter flings a bullet belt as he wraps it around his body near Maidan Shahr village, west of Kabul, November 18, 2001.

Shamil Zhumatov

A woman carries her son in her arms and a bucket on her head in Kumkishlyak refugee camp in northern Afghanistan, November 3, 2001. Humanitarian groups urged the United States in its military campaign to avoid worsening the plight of refugees already suffering from hunger and drought.

Shamil Zhumatov

Wearing the all-enveloping blue burqa, three Afghan women carry laundry as they walk along the Kabul River, December 7, 2001. The Taliban's rule over its last bastion in Kandahar in southern Afghanistan came to an end on that day.

Peter Andrews

A family rides their horse-and-cart through a battle-damaged area of the city of
Kabul, December 7, 2001.

Peter Andrews

Peter Andrews

An amputee, followed by his wife wearing a burqa, walks down a street in Kabul, December 6, 2001. To war-weary Afghans, amputees are a common sight because of the millions of land mines scattered across the country after decades of fighting.

Madina, an Afghan woman who is unsure of her own age, holds her son in their refugee home in a suburb of Kabul, December 8, 2001.

Damir Sagolj

A Northern Alliance soldier rests on the front line at the border of Kunduz province, the last province in northern Afghanistan to fall from Taliban control, November 24, 2001. That day about 600 pro-Taliban fighters surrendered as their forces crumbled under the U.S.-led campaign.

Gleb Garanich

An elderly man brandishes an assault rifle which he vows to use against Americans, October 2, 2001. Prior to U.S. air raids launched on Afghanistan five days later, Taliban officials appealed to the Afghans to fight any invasion force.

Sayed Salahuddin

A Northern Alliance fighter armed with an AK-47 assault rifle scans Taliban positions at a front-line observation post in Bakhshi i Khel, north of the Afghan capital Kabul, October 26, 2001.

Yannis Behrakis

Adrees Latif

It was the first day of Ramadan, the holy month when Muslims fast from sunrise to sunset, as we made our way back to Quetta after spending all day taking photographs in the Pakistani border town of Chaman. Afghan refugee families given shelter in Pakistan were preparing what food they had to break the day's fast. As the sun went down, we found ourselves at a military checkpoint southeast of Chaman. It was in these mountains where I broke my fast with sweet bread, dates, and green tea offered by travelling Afghan Pashtuns.

As the sky changed color from magenta to dark blue, the nearly dozen people gathered and laid cloth on the mountainside to pray facing Mecca. At this moment I found myself searching for an image that would capture the essence of the holy month.

As the crescent moon appeared in the darkening sky, I raced to capture an Afghan Pashtun bowing in prayer as the moon shone behind him. As the Pashtun, later identified as Afghan refugee Shear Jaan, ended his formal prayer, he then raised his hands in front of his face in a silent prayer. As I saw the man pray through my camera, I could only imagine that his prayers reflected the same sentiment of hope for Afghanistan that I found in everyone I encountered.

Adrees Latif

Afghan women wait for distribution
of humanitarian aid in Kabul, December
4, 2001.

Damir Sagolj

The Graveyard of Invaders

Brian Williams
Mikhail Evstafiev
Sayed Salahuddin

If you managed to look your enemy in the eye, you had come close to dying yourself.

Reuters photographer, Mikhail Evstafiev

When you're wounded and left on Afghanistan's plains
And the women come out to cut up what remains,
Just roll to your rifle and blow out your brains
And go to your God like a soldier.

Rudyard Kipling

The Soviet invasion in 1979 opened a new chapter in the bloody history of Afghanistan. The Cold War occupation turned into the Soviet Union's Vietnam and was a first fatal step toward the unraveling of a once-mighty empire. In this chapter, a Reuters photographer who had served with the Soviet military and two Reuters correspondents describe their involvement in their own words.

Mikhail Evstafiev, then a 24-year-old Soviet officer and now a Reuters photojournalist in Washington, D.C., writes:

For a Soviet soldier arriving in Afghanistan, the flight into Kabul airport was unforgettable. A sudden gut-wrenching nose dive as the aircraft strained in a tight corkscrew, then shot off bright flares to protect itself from attack by Stinger missiles supplied by the Americans to mujahideen fighters. The dramatic maneuver took just minutes, as if the pilot, ignoring the whirring dials on the instrument panel of the Ilyushin-72 transport plane, were in a terrible rush to escape these moments of intense danger.

Once at Kabul airport and with the ramp finally down, the beauty of the landscape was overwhelming. But the rapture soon surrendered to other emotions, when the realities and dangers of war triumphed over the magnificent mountains and green valleys. As we bundled off the plane with our packs, we knew we were not on a tourist trip to this country.

I arrived in Afghanistan on one of these Il-72s, nicknamed "cattle carriers," in January of 1987, a fresh lieutenant who for romantic and patriotic reasons volunteered to fight in Afghanistan and back its Communist-inspired revolution. My term of duty covered two years, enough to witness the unspeakable horror of battle, the tragic loss of close comrades, and the final days of withdrawal.

It took a few months to adjust to service in Afghanistan. Getting used to the unknown culture and tongue was gradual. There were shocking battle stories from combat veterans, and the climate was harsh—freezing in winter and sweltering in summer. For the Soviet patrols, the terrain and the weather would sometimes turn out to be as formidable a foe as the fierce and elusive mujahideen warriors.

Then there was combat. The smell of gunpowder that filled your nose and lungs and the acrid, sticky smell of death were reminders that until your term was over, you needed to stay focused and cover your back. There were no friends except your comrades. In firefights, you knew that if you

managed to look your enemy in the eye, you had come close to dying yourself.

For as long as the war in Afghanistan lasted—nearly a decade—very little was known in the Soviet Union about what really went on there. Going in, I didn't know what to expect. I had scant knowledge of the country, just the basic facts—the geography and the history. The official reasons for being there were repeated over and over like a mantra by my government.

Short reports about Afghanistan in the Soviet media, if any at all, were upbeat and focused on humanitarian aid to the "southern neighbor." Sometimes they referred to clashes between "Afghan revolutionary forces" and the "dushman," or enemy of the new Kabul regime. The reports emphasized that the "Limited Contingent of Soviet Troops" was in Afghanistan for a just cause, to perform its "international duty."

At home in the Soviet Union, veterans of the Afghan war kept their emotions and memories to themselves. They said little or nothing about their experiences, except perhaps in a circle of close friends, fellow "afghantsi"—those who had served there, those who could understand.

Soon I could see why. Afghanistan and the life back home were worlds apart. Without media attention, few knew, few cared about the war in this distant and troubled land.

Life took on a different meaning for us in Afghanistan. We felt very much on our own there. In the first few months young soldiers might have held idealistic views. Some saw their mission as to help "progressive Afghans" build a better future and fight off the Islamic fundamentalists.

After a while, though, you came to understand that your main objective was to stay alive and make sure the men under your command also survived to go home to their families.

But for some soldiers the war became an addiction. Officers would even go back for a second term, because they felt they were missing out on something. The Afghan battlefield had become their home.

The "doohee," Russian slang for the "dushman" or enemy, which also means ghost, were everywhere. Some were well equipped and trained in special camps in Pakistan by Western instructors. Some were just "off the fields" with nothing but a pair of sandals and a great determination to fight a holy war and become martyrs. The "doohee" knew they didn't stand a chance against a modern army, so they mastered guerrilla warfare techniques: They lived in our shadows, blending with the inhospitable landscape, often invisible to the outsider's eye, posing as peasants and hiding their guns until nightfall.

One thing any Soviet soldier dreaded was capture by the mujahideen. The options were conversion to Islam or gruesome torture and death. The Geneva Convention did not apply to the mujahideen. The first thing any conscript heard was terrifying tales of Soviet prisoners being skinned alive or having their eyes gouged out with bayonets. We saw the "doohee" as primitive nomads who regarded life as cheap.

When it came to fighting, many of them proved to be fearless warriors, but in my unit we never thought of them as unconquerable. They were simply an enemy that the Soviet army must defeat. We never really lost a major

battle, but every day the enemy seemed to reappear like ghosts. They operated in tight groups, enough to destroy a small Soviet convoy in a remote area or attack an outpost.

At first our generals had expected to pacify the country, securing key cities, towns, airports, and the roads that linked them with minimal casualties and without encountering significant resistance. The generals soon learned, however, that that was not enough. The traditional warrior society could deliver crippling punches. Our military operations were preceded by massive shows of firepower from aircraft and artillery. But this was not the conventional Cold War confrontation that the generals had tactics worked out for.

We knew that our Spetsnaz special forces had the upper hand with their rigorous training and helicopters. Their dangerous and secret missions were breaking the back of the mujahideen by attacking their camps, cutting off their supply of arms, and killing their field commanders. The word Spetsnaz made the mujahideen shiver with fear.

In daytime the Soviet forces and the Afghan allies would rule most of the roads and central towns. But as darkness fell, all traffic would stop and the "doohee" took over. They seemed to sense our weakest spots and always struck when we least expected—using ambushes, land mines, and even knives if they could get close enough. The "doohee" were masters of hit-and-run attacks. They knew that Soviet retaliation was swift and deadly, so they would kill and then flee for their lives.

Most of my comrades, surprisingly enough, dreamed of combat and considered themselves lucky to leave base and set out on a mission. Not all would come back. The corpses of the fallen were taken home in zinc caskets on transport planes that we called the Black Tulips. As battles became fiercer and each side threw in new weapons, our casualties mounted, reaching nearly 15,000 dead over the decade we were there.

Many were the soldiers I served alongside who never made it back alive. I sometimes wonder how, with all those close calls, my life was spared. Perhaps I was given a chance to live on so I could describe the war, which remained a mystery to many who weren't there.

After combat operations at our bases, despite a strict "dry law" imposed on the troops, officers would stand up in silence and raise the traditional "third toast" to those who never came back. In the barracks, soldiers would leave the bunks of fallen comrades vacant in their memory. Obelisks with names and photographs of fallen Soviet servicemen could be seen along almost every road in Afghanistan. When we pulled out, we took them all home, so that they would not be desecrated by the enemy.

Being disciplined soldiers, we obeyed our orders to the letter; we fought without asking questions or doubting the mission that was to be carried out. It was bad to take doubts into battle. Yet as the war dragged on, some of us wondered how we suddenly found ourselves in a conflict that appeared endless.

To us it seemed that most educated Afghans, mainly from the big cities, supported the revolution and the political course of the new regime in Kabul, as well as the Soviet role in the conflict, fearing the Islamic religious grip. Unfortunately for us, however, the majority of poor Afghans, living in primitive mud huts in a lifestyle almost unchanged from the Middle Ages, saw the Soviets as infidels and invaders. We also knew all too well that even for the fearsome British army, Afghanistan had lived up to its reputation as the graveyard of invaders.

As genuine as the intentions of the new Moscow-backed Afghan government might have been, they coincided with a clash of bigger interests. A new Cold War chapter was unfolding in the region. Washington supported what we regarded as Islamic fundamentalism. Moscow supported the revolutionary regime in Kabul, which the West branded as "Marxist" and thus "another threat to the world."

By February 15, 1989, the last Soviet forces would leave Afghanistan. There was never talk among the soldiers, then or later, about losing the war, as there was never talk about winning it. We believed that we had performed our so-called "international duty," had trained and equipped the Afghan army, and had won all our battles. We were proud of the medals we received and never let anyone cast a shadow on our comrades' heroic deeds.

Going home, my friends and I were young officers; we expected a great future, a brand-new life ahead. What we found in the Soviet Union turned out to be devastating. The peace of mind which every soldier hoped for proved elusive for many. Some of us found we no longer fitted into our previous lives. We felt nostalgic for the snow-peaked mountains of Afghanistan, but there was no going back.

Thousands of Soviet soldiers and officers who came back from Afghanistan to an "ideal" called the Soviet Union were uncomfortable with the system they had once loved and praised. They returned to a god called Communism that they now found hollow, to a regime that was aging and weak, to a country that had little to offer to the casualties of war and did everything to hide the truth about Afghanistan.

The morning after Christmas Day, 1979, an eight-year-old boy was sent out onto Kabul's snow-covered streets by his father to buy bread. He was confronted by a rumbling Soviet armored column.

The shivering boy was Sayed Salahuddin, who is now the Reuters Kabul bureau chief. Sayed lived through the Soviet occupation and the reign of the Taliban and reported nonstop on events in Afghanistan after September 11.

He remembers listening with his father and uncles throughout that Christmas night to overseas radio broadcasts of the Soviet invasion of their land.

The next morning when I was sent out to buy bread, there was already a column of Russian tanks and trucks in our street. There was apprehension about what had happened but not fear.

Russians on the tanks were giving out biscuits, chocolates, and chewing gum to passersby like me.

Other Russian tanks had taken up positions at key traffic circles, and Russian soldiers with Afghans by their side were directing traffic.

But within weeks life in Kabul appeared to have slipped back to almost normal. You saw Russians in the bazaars—they were the shopkeepers' best customers. But they weren't aggressive in public.

The biggest change was in the shops. Suddenly there was vodka for sale everywhere. Shop windows were full of Russian clothing—caps and uniforms—which soldiers had sold to get money to buy vodka and hashish and Afghan curios.

I only realized how dramatic an event the invasion was when I walked past the Presidential Palace one day and saw it was guarded by Russians. If even the president of our country had to be guarded by Russians, I knew something was wrong.

In 1981 Brian Williams, who had covered the wars in Vietnam and Cambodia, arrived in Islamabad, Pakistan, the Reuters reporting base for the conflict in Afghanistan. Soviet officials had put the country off-limits to non-Communist journalists when the war was in full swing. He found a city abuzz with spies and rumors. By the time he left three years later the powerful Soviet army in neighboring Afghanistan was out of its depth.

In a quiet week leading up to December 25, 1979, the only major international news was the signing of a cease-fire in Rhodesia's independence guerrilla war. But on Christmas Day, the news tempo dramatically changed. While celebrations were in full swing, Soviet tanks and troops crossed into Afghanistan, thereby taking the first fatal step toward the unravelling of the mighty Soviet empire and at least in some way setting the scene for the events of September 11.

Gorbachev, Yeltsin, the Berlin Wall—they are the usual signposts on the road to the breakup of the Soviet Union.

But what if Afghanistan had remained just a stop on the Hippie Trail, a faraway land known mainly through the poetry and derring-do tales of Britain's imperial writer Rudyard Kipling?

What if the Soviet leaders, instead of pouring thousands of troops into Afghanistan over the next 10 years in a fruitless bid to win Kipling's ageless Great Game, had simply allowed Afghanistan to remain lost in time?

Would there have been a September 11 attack, an Osama bin Laden, a Mullah Mohammad Omar?

Would there still be a Soviet Union?

If Vietnam was America's quagmire that for years drained the nation's soul, Afghanistan was a quagmire that sucked the heart out of the Soviet Union.

More than anything, the failure of the war in Afghanistan opened people's eyes, both back home in Russia and abroad, to a Soviet system that could no longer deliver on the battlefield or ensure the well-being of its own people. A world superpower, fighting on its own doorstep, could not defeat a disorganized, ragtag army of mujahideen who mainly still lived a feudal way of life from centuries ago.

The Soviet soldiers marching into Afghanistan could not have known that among their foes in Afghanistan were Saudi-born Osama bin Laden and thousands of other non-Afghanis drawn to the conflict because the infidel Russians had taken over a Muslim country.

While these non-Afghanis brought much aid and money from their homelands, they were barely bit players on the battlefields of Afghanistan at that time. In military terms, they were hardly mentioned in dispatches.

My first impressions on arriving in Islambad were that the wild and lawless Pakistani-Afghan border and the neatly laid out Pakistani capital of Islamabad, with its endless round of diplomatic cocktail parties, were settings where Kipling would have thrived.

Spies—Russian, American, British, Chinese, German, Indian, Pakistani, and who knows from what other countries—prowled the area in many guises, all asking the same questions: Who is winning the war? Who is going to win?

In 1981 no one was certain. But even by the time I left in 1983, well before the Kremlin back in Moscow admitted it, everyone—including the Russians on the ground—knew the answers.

The Russians could not last in Afghanistan, and only two questions remained: When would they withdraw and who would replace them?

At the time I arrived there was a confidence, even a cockiness, in Russian officials when they discussed the war. By 1984—five years before the final withdrawal—the mood had changed to near-desperation.

As Soviet forces stalled in their fight to control the rugged Afghanistan terrain, the Russians in Pakistan were pressured by Moscow for intelligence on the once-dismissed mujahideen groups that had mainly based themselves in Pakistan's northern city of Peshawar.

Subtle questioning gave way to near-pleas from Russians for any scrap of information that could be sent back to Moscow to show they were doing their job. The agony went on until February 1989, when the last Soviet troops crossed the Oxus River on Afghanistan's northern border back into the Soviet Union.

The cost in lives and money was enormous. The Soviet casualties numbered 15,000, and nearly 50,000 Soviet troops were wounded during their time in Afghanistan. On the Afghan side, according to some estimates, more than one million died, and many more were wounded. Four to five million people were driven into exile, most of them arriving in neighboring Pakistan and Iran.

Although the Soviet troop strength of around 100,000 was nearly five times less than the number of Americans who fought in Vietnam, they were spread over a country five times the size of Vietnam. During 10 years of war more than 500,000 mainly conscript Soviet soldiers rotated through Afghanistan. Many came home unwounded but often with debilitating illnesses and nearly all sick at heart from what they had been through.

What Reuters photographer Mikhail Evstafiev and his fellow returnees found back home was an economy approaching the abyss, few jobs to go to, and a nation in ferment that seemed to have lost its way.

The Afghan War had drawn billions of dollars away each year from an already creaking Soviet economy, denying urgently needed money to improve industries and to better people's living conditions. Up to three billion dollars a year went to propping up the Soviet-installed Kabul government; another billion a year went to paying the salaries of troops. Other costs of running the war over the 10 years were estimated at 30 times more.

Was the Soviet Union wrong to care so much about the fate of Afghanistan and to become so deeply involved? In the eyes of most Russian strategists—and even some neutral observers—not to have cared about a country on its own borders would have been criminal. The mistake was in becoming so deeply and hopelessly involved in Afghanistan when, though there was instability, the main fighting, ironically, was among fellow Communists for power.

For centuries, from the Tsars to the Communist Party chiefs in the Kremlin, Afghanistan had been a buffer state against attack from enemies and a magnet, some say, for Moscow's ambition to open a path to a warm-water port on the Indian Ocean in neighboring Pakistan. In 1979 it was the buffer-state argument, rather than the dream of a warm-water port, that was in vogue in the corridors of Soviet power.

The official Soviet justification for the invasion was that political instability sweeping Afghanistan was poised to spill over and undermine Moscow's neighboring Central Asian Republics.

Only later in the 1990s, when top-secret Politburo papers about the Soviet decision to intervene in Afghanistan became public knowledge, did the painful agonizing among the leadership become clear.

When he came to power, Mikhail Gorbachev, the first new-generation Soviet leader, swiftly saw the writing on the wall. In February 1986 he went public with his concern, delivering a speech at the 27th Congress of the Communist Party of the Soviet Union that described Afghanistan as a "bleeding wound" and signaled that the Soviet Union was planning to withdraw.

But even if the Russian bear was going home, the West was going to make it as painful as possible. The Russians were all too aware that the United States viewed the Soviet-Afghan War as an opportunity to exact revenge for its own humiliation in Vietnam. For years the United States, under Cold War warrior Ronald Reagan, and other Western-allied nations had been supplying the mujahideen with hundreds of millions of dollars in weapons and aid.

By 1984 Reagan was already authorizing military supplies to the mujahideen of nearly $250 million a month. The following year he raised the stakes further by authorizing the supply of Stinger ground-to-air missiles and the training of the mujahideen to use them. The Afghans fired their first Stingers at Soviet aircraft during late 1986, and from that moment the Soviets lost their one trump card in the war—air power.

They were soon losing helicopters and planes regularly and could no longer rely on helping ground forces with air cover. It is estimated that nearly 1,000 Stingers were supplied to the mujahideen.

Looking back at the conflict, Ian Kemp, a military expert from *Jane's Defence Weekly*, said the invasion was doomed because the Soviets tried to fight a conventional war based on set-piece battles from World War II and strategies evolved for mass army clashes in the Cold War. "The Soviets sent some of their best troops into Afghanistan but they were organized exclusively for mechanized warfare with heavy reliance on weapons like tanks," Kemp said. The agile mujahideen relied on their age-old tactics of ambushes and surprise.

Comparing the Soviet debacle and the US success in swiftly ousting Afghanistan's Taliban rulers, military experts said the United States set its sights lower, made better use of Afghan allies as proxy fighters, put greater efforts into intelligence gathering, capitalized on high tech weapons systems, and concentrated on using air strikes. The introduction of Stingers had sealed the Soviets' fate.

Put simply, Moscow invaded Afghanistan with the intention of occupying the country, a far more demanding task than Washington set itself.

David Jordan, a lecturer in Defence Studies at London's King's College, said Soviet failures were the keys to American success. "Essentially, the Americans learnt from the Soviets." Just as America's failure to win hearts and minds in Vietnam had led to their downfall there, so the Soviets paid a similiar price in Afghanistan. "All the factions put their differences aside and turned their animosity full blast on the invaders."

A Soviet soldier overlooks a mountain pass as a convoy of troops heads out for a combat operation in Afghanistan, 1987. The rugged terrain made such convoys vulnerable to ambush.

Mikhail Evstafiev

Mikhail Evstafiev

A Soviet Mi-8 helicopter delivers supplies to an outpost near Kabul, 1988.

Mikhail Evstafiev

Kabul airport, autumn of 1988. In a few months the Soviet war in Afghanistan would be over. After agreements were signed in Geneva, Soviet troops were withdrawing. The pull-out was going smoothly, in a well-organized way, by land and by air.

I was an officer in the Soviet Army and by that time had spent a full two years in Afghanistan. As soldiers, we didn't feel that we had lost the war, but we didn't talk about victory either. We just accepted the fact that our mission in Afghanistan was over.

All the major battles were now things of the past. Yet the enemy was still active, the mujahideen regrouping for a final face-off with the regime in Kabul. There was talk they would strike our troops as we left.

Crack Spetsnaz units, or Soviet special forces, operated from Kabul airport. Acting on intelligence, highly trained operatives flew secret helicopter missions to intercept arms, to destroy hideouts and enemy bases.

I flew on several missions with them. The group in this picture had just returned to the airport after one such mission. It struck me how relaxed and casual the men looked, as if this were a regular 9-to-5 job, or a routine assignment. As if there were no war around us. We spoke later about the war and their feelings. Some said: "Enough. Time to go home." Others said: "We haven't yet avenged our dead friends, but how long can this go on?"

No one wanted to die; the finish line was so close, almost visible ahead. Yet someone had to risk his life on a daily basis to make sure the others made it back safely.

Photographing this Spetsnaz unit; I reflected that these soldiers were just a bunch of kids a couple of years ago, and now they were grown men who had seen it all. I thought going home for them would be joyful. For a battle-hardened special forces soldier, though, adapting to a humdrum life without war could itself be an ordeal. Looking at this photograph, I often wonder: Have all of them managed to adjust to their new realities? Have they found peace within themselves after all that they went through? Have I?

Mikhail Evstafiev

Officers and soldiers of the 103rd
Airborne Division keep watch on a hill
in Afghanistan in 1988.

Mikhail Evstafiev

Afghan troops loyal to the Moscow-backed regime sit on a tank during a combat operation in Afghanistan. Undated.

Mikhail Evstafiev

A Soviet soldier mans a position at a garrison in Kabul, 1988.

Mikhail Evstafiev

Mikhail Evstafiev

Empty shells at a firing range of a Soviet outpost near Kabul, 1988.

General Boris Gromov, the last commander of the 40th Army in Afghanistan, salutes during a ceremony in Moscow in 1993.

Mikhail Evstafiev

Mikhail Evstafiev

Soldiers prepare to board an IL-76 transport plane during the final phase of the Soviet troop withdrawal at Kabul airport, January 1988.

Soviet troops cross over a bridge from Afghanistan into the town of Termez, USSR, during the last day of the withdrawal of Soviet forces from Afghanistan, February 15, 1989. The armored personnel carrier flies the forces' colors. The withdrawing soldiers were given a warm welcome by family members and military and local officials.

Mikhail Evstafiev

Life Under the Taliban

Sayed Salahuddin

"Imagine if they actually did it," one of us said. We laughed, knowing it was too ridiculous to contemplate. And then they did it.

Sayed Salahuddin
on the Taliban's destruction
of the giant Bamiyan Buddhas

It was the autumn of 1994 when I saw my first Taliban. They were sitting on the roof of a building beside a road leading to the southern city of Kandahar. They looked meek and unassuming. They had assault rifles slung over their shoulders, but that was hardly unusual in Afghanistan, where many men carry a Kalashnikov as if it were a fashion accessory. They were polite but shy of my camera as they lounged in this isolated sector of the former royal capital. What was unusal about the scene was the traffic. It was running smoothly and unhindered. This highway was free of the armed bandits who prowled the rest of the country, demanding payment from every passing vehicle, cyclist, or pedestrian. In some places the payoffs to these robbers were as regular as toll booths on a highway.

The Taliban set out to restore peace, to establish law and order, to cleanse the land of debauchery, and to eradicate theft, rape, and warlords. In doing so, they also banned lipstick, music, and playing cards and were known to interrupt football matches to stage impromptu executions between the goalposts.

In that time and place, their exploits swiftly became the stuff of legend. Afghanistan had deteriorated into a mosaic of fiefdoms ruled by power-hungry tribal chieftains and battle-hardened veterans of the mujahideen struggle. Bandits preyed on travellers, rape was common, and theft a fact of life. The struggle for power among rival mujahideen factions had fractured the country, leaving some battle-weary citizens even yearning for the relative tranquillity of the Soviet occupation. The government operated in name only.

I had grown up under the Soviet occupation and started university in Kabul the year before Moscow finally pulled its tanks out in 1989. I came from a typical middle-class Afghan family—at least typical of the time. One of my sisters had a university degree; two were teachers. I always wore Western clothes. With my friends I listened to music, chatted with girls, and enjoyed mixed picnics and parties. I also was eager for peace.

When I travelled to Kandahar and first encountered these quiet Taliban, I was with a British colleague and we wanted to interview Mullah Mohammad Omar, the reclusive spiritual leader of this new movement. But he turned us down. He did not want to meet a Westerner, his aides said. We were disappointed, but we had no reason to think that the Taliban would ever be a major force beyond the city of Kandahar. The mujahideen who ruled the rest of the country appeared far too formidable for these young upstarts, most from the ethnic Pashtun group that was dominant in the south.

Here in their southern stronghold they were clearly popular. "They are angels," said one driver. For him the Taliban crackdown on crime spelled an end to highway robbery. "I wish they would take the whole country so that we don't have to worry about security and these armed gangs any more," the elderly man said.

Within days of our departure, his dream began to come true. The vast southern province of Kandahar fell into the hands of the turbaned Taliban. Now the name is associated indelibly with evil, but in those days Taliban, "knowledge seekers" in Arabic, embodied the message of hope that the word represented. Their battle cry when they first leapt onto the Afghan stage was to save the people from petty warlords and lawlessness and to establish security throughout the land. They had no desire for power, they said. They would not keep power, they said. And we believed them.

Their message resonated among Afghans. People from all walks of life were exhausted by 13 years of Soviet-backed rule followed by two years of mujahideen government marked by constant battles for power in which civilians were the chief casualties. People wanted the rule of law, regardless of who provided it. We saw the Taliban as our salvation.

One of their first acts in Kandahar was to hang the bodies of several local mujahideen commanders accused of various crimes, most especially of rape, from the barrel of a tank turret. It was a deterrent that put an immediate halt to road robbery. Aid convoys suddenly found that they were no longer stopped on the road by armed gangs and looted. Trade—the lifeline of Afghanistan since it had figured as a major stop on the ancient Silk Road—began to revive.

The Taliban's early edicts, which struck many people in the West as "excesses," did not seem that intolerable. Compulsory burqas? The overwhelming majority of women in the areas the Taliban controlled wore burqas anyway. Compulsory beards? Most Afghan men had beards—no matter how wispy. It was a cultural custom, not a religious rite. The Taliban were only implementing a length directive, we thought. People began to pin their confidence on the Taliban. They were a beacon of hope, and their numbers swelled with young men joining the ranks of their swift and almost bloodless advance.

I was among those seduced by the promise of a return to orderly society. I allowed myself to dream of a growing economy, more job opportunities, and the reconstruction of a country over which foreign powers had fought proxy wars since 1978. For the first time I felt that if the Taliban came to Kabul, I could start to look forward to a brighter future. It was time for peace. I, and many others, believed the Taliban might be able to provide it.

They were to surprise everyone. In a few short weeks, and with little resistance from local commanders, the Taliban extended their rule over large swathes of the Pashtun belt in southern Afghanistan. They swiftly won the sympathies of a populace yearning for a government that would put the interests of its citizens first.

By the winter of 1995, the Taliban were encamped outside the gates of Kabul. It was there that they encountered their first real resistance from the rival mujahideen forces entrenched in the capital. They responded in a way that marked them out as being no different from any other of Afghanistan's warmongers. And I felt my first reservations.

For three years, the mujahideen parties had been squabbling in Kabul, raining rockets down on the city, reducing whole suburbs to rubble and killing tens of thousands of civilians as they battled for the top jobs in the government. The most powerful of these rivals was a group composed of ethnic Tajiks from the north, and they united in the face of the common enemy and fought off the Taliban with spirit.

I was out of the country when that first battle for Kabul was fought. I could scarcely believe it when I returned to find that, after failing to take the city peaceably, the Taliban, "the knowledge seekers," had adopted the same tactics as their enemy. They were shelling the city indiscriminately. Civilians were being killed again. Then they resorted to one of the traditional tactics of any Afghan war—take advantage of differences and divisions within their enemy and buy off individual commanders. On a September night in 1996 they swept into Kabul without a shot being fired as the mujahideen retreated to the north.

Residents of Kabul awoke the next day relieved that the city had not been the scene of a bloodbath. They also awoke to wonder what was in store for them under the rule of these fervent young men in their black turbans and with their ardor for Islam. They hoped for peace above all, but there were shocks in store.

The grisly sight that met the people of Kabul on that first morning was the body of the last Communist president, Najibullah, hanging from an overhead traffic post along with that of his brother. Najibullah was not loved. He was nicknamed "the butcher" for his arrest and killing of scores of resistance fighters and Islamic faithful during the days of Soviet occupation. No one mourned him, but the street was hushed outside the Presidential Palace where the bodies hung. Onlookers spoke in whispers, looking with a mix of horror and surprise at the bloodstained bodies. The Taliban had stuffed cigarettes into their fingers and Afghani bills into their pockets to represent what they most opposed—debauchery and corruption.

Reaction on the street to the fate handed out to Najibullah was neutral. People watched. But within hours the Taliban stunned the city as they began issuing edicts to impose their own brand of Islam—Mullah Omar's interpretation that sought to reproduce in Afghanistan an imagined seventh-century utopia. Mullah Omar wanted to take Afghanistan back in time. If their killing of Najibullah was dramatic, their next move was scarcely less so.

The first Taliban edicts banned women from working and then from schools and colleges. Imagine the conversation around my family dinner table with a university-educated sister and another who was a teacher. We were outraged, and so were most of our friends. But we still harbored the hope that the Taliban might make good on their promise to liberate the country, wipe the slate clean, and then melt back into the shadows.

But other edicts followed. Bans were imposed on, among other things, photography, movies, neckties, television, and makeup. Images of living things were banned, based on the Taliban's interpretation of the Koran's outlawing of icons. Music, except for capella religious chants, was forbidden as decadent. Overnight, traditional music and much-loved Indian Bollywood movie tunes vanished. That wasn't all that disappeared. Women did, too, behind their burqas.

At first some of the more outrageous edicts were simply ignored by a populace accustomed to capricious rulers. But when they saw their draconian laws being ignored, the Taliban cracked down, and so was born the Ministry for Promotion of Virtue and Prevention of Vice—better known as the religious police. It was their job to enforce restrictions banning Western clothes, to ensure that women were veiled from head to toe when venturing outdoors, and to beat those whose heels click-clacked on the street.

The religious police were the most feared and powerful tool of the Taliban. They became such a byword for terror that parents would frighten their children into obedience and scare them from going out into the street by saying a religious police patrol was out and about.

Their squads, sometimes armed with whips or even guns, patrolled the cities in vehicles with loudspeakers blaring religious exhortations. Men who trimmed their beards too short were jailed until their facial hair could be grasped in a fist. Prayer became compulsory—traffic was stopped in the streets when the muezzin's call went out. Public lashings became commonplace. Thieves had limbs amputated; serious criminals were executed. Crowds of up to 20,000 people—including dozens of women and children—would gather to watch the punishments, some with horror, some with amusement.

Many of us still believed the reign of the Taliban was only temporary. As soon as they finished off the mujahideen—now united into the Northern Alliance—they would disappear as they had pledged, or so we thought. The strict rules, we told ourselves, were necessary to maintain the discipline of the Taliban ranks, to focus Taliban minds on the task ahead. We kept our opinions about the edicts to ourselves, prepared to put up with the harsh conditions now in return for a better society tomorrow. "We are here to rule people's hearts through leniency rather than force," read a huge Taliban slogan inscribed on a Kabul wall. It seemed little could be further from the truth.

They did not rule our hearts, but they ruled our lives.

I got married. Our wedding ceremony was more like a funeral. Afghan weddings are traditionally gay affairs, but ours had no music, no chattering of men and women in a room together, no dancing, and no video of the happy bride and groom. My sister braved much to sneak in a camera and record that day.

It quickly became apparent that not all Taliban leaders believed they had to obey their own strictures. I found out about Taliban officials who watched videos, listened to music, even drank alcohol. Some sent their daughters to school and university in Pakistan and made sure their sons escaped being recruited for frontline duty against the Northern Alliance. The religious police simply turned a blind eye.

I learned that the head of the military tribunal had been bribed to helped a pair of convicted murderers to flee Afghanistan. Others were executed in their place. He was removed from his job after news of his corruption circulated, but he was never punished.

Enforcement of the Taliban edicts lacked consistency. In the cities, the religious police were vigilant and intransigent. In the countryside, some women walked without the burqa and worked in the fields. Sometimes I dared to raise the issue with the religious police. I was swiftly silenced and accused of being a propaganda tool for the West. "Women in the countryside don't use makeup so they are not as seductive as the women in the cities," one religious policeman told me. "Do you understand?"

As a journalist, my own difficulties began as I tried to report on Taliban rule. Their ban on television and pictures meant that every day I had to act with extreme caution, snatching photographs when backs were turned, making sure I asked permission whenever I thought I was in an awkward position. I could get away with it, but only with difficulty, and there were risks. One of my most alarming moments was in 1998 after the bombings of the U.S. embassies in Kenya and Tanzania, when the United States bombarded suspected training camps of Osama bin Laden in eastern Khost with cruise missiles. Trying to get near the site, I was detained in eastern Afghanistan with three colleagues. Our captors accused us of being spies for the CIA. They held us four days, slapping us and threatening that we could be tried for espionage and face the death penalty. Only when our credentials were confirmed by Kabul were we quietly released.

Taliban officials frequently warned me that my reporting was angering their superiors. Sometimes they were direct; sometimes the mere fact that they were unavailable signalled their displeasure.

As a family we debated whether to leave. My instinct told me to stay. I wanted to see what happened next. One day I realized that out of 70 fellow university graduates from my final year, only three of us remained in the country. I stayed.

Increasingly, I felt that the "knowledge seekers" were tarnishing the image not only of Islam but of Afghans. They were using Islam to enhance their own vested interests, and they showed little tolerance. They saw the world in black and white. Orders were orders. Don't argue. Obey.

The treatment of women was a flashpoint for much discontent. True, women were no longer raped or kidnapped in Afghanistan, but then these are crimes not tolerated in any corner of the world. People began to murmur. "We would not mind about most of the restrictions if the Taliban at least realized the need of our society and allowed women to work and study. We could put up with the burqa and the beard restrictions," a friend told me. Even among ministers, doubts were voiced about the ban on women working. The majority of women in a land of war and widows were the breadwinners for their families. Taking away their ability to work deprived them of a livelihood. Some resorted to prostitution to survive, or begged in the streets. "Do we want this?" Mullah Khaksar, the Taliban's deputy interior minister once asked me, echoing the thoughts of a growing number of his colleagues. "Omar just wants to conquer and rule. He wants to be tough and is a dictator," Khaksar said.

The religious police grew even harsher when Taliban fighters suffered military setbacks in the north. When several thousand Taliban were massacred in non-Pashtun areas, their colleagues retaliated by killing civilians. They razed to the ground several villages near the front line north of Kabul. Acts like these stoked hatred of the Taliban in their distinctive turbans and shalwar-kameez—a loose tunic and baggy trousers that by Taliban law had to end above the ankle. Resentment also mounted at the foreigners—known by most people as Arabs—who swelled the Taliban ranks. We gradually became aware that these foreigners were loyal to bin Laden and were the most fearsome and most extreme allies of the Taliban.

I witnessed the modus operandi of these foreign fighters first hand in August 1999 at a Taliban position in the battle zone to the north of Kabul. I spotted a group of Taliban near a small village and stopped to get information on the latest developments in the fighting. I saw a young villager being interrogated by several armed Pakistanis with an Afghan Talib interpreting for them. The barefoot villager, who looked to be in his early 30s, said he was not a combatant but just an onlooker. He pleaded to be freed. The Pakistanis barely listened. In less than a minute one Pakistani ordered that he be killed. I was still wondering what I could to do to help him when the gunshots of his executioners rang out.

I knew I was in danger myself. As I tried to walk away, one of the Taliban stopped me and asked who I was. I said I worked for Reuters, without spelling out that it was a foreign news agency, but assuming that he would know. In those few seconds I thought he would tell the Pakistanis that I worked for a Western news agency and that they would kill me on the spot for witnessing their killing of an Afghan. But the Talib had understood me to say that I worked for the Taliban's Bakhtar news agency. He told me to leave, quickly. I left.

The influence of the al Qaeda foreigners in my country grew stronger and stronger. It began to dawn on me just how much of a rogue state my homeland had become. It wasn't such a bad feeling. I thought that change was now becoming inevitable.

For many, the Taliban's destruction of the ancient Buddha statues at Bamiyan in March 2001 was the final straw. One senior Taliban official leaked news of the plan to me weeks in advance, hoping that the news would provoke such outrage that the 1,000-year-old figures might be saved. For a while, as protests poured in from around the world, with international anger grabbing headlines, I thought his strategy had worked. My Kabul peers discussed the fate of the statues every day like a soap opera plot. "Imagine if they actually did it," one of us said. We laughed at the absurdity of the deed. And then the Taliban went ahead and did it.

Many Afghans were just as outraged as anyone in the international community. There was no justification for such vandalism. Days afterward, another Taliban official told me privately that he would rather have watched his son's head blown from his shoulders than have seen the Buddhas blasted into eternity.

Within months, the United States launched its war on the Taliban and al Qaeda. The Taliban tried not to show their fear. But one incident was revealing. It was a fine autumn day, and I saw a tank manned by several Taliban rolling down the street. I asked if I could take their photograph, and they laughingly agreed. I got out of my car to get a good frame. Suddenly the driver accelerated, roared forward, and crushed my car. The driver leapt out just in time. The Taliban raced off down the street roaring with delight. I decided this wasn't road rage. They were nervous and didn't like me, or perhaps they just couldn't control their own tank. It did not bode well, I felt, for their fate in a war.

Ironically, I detected the end of the Taliban, when it came, through the religious police. On November 12, the day before Kabul fell, I drove out toward the front line to shoot some video of bomb damage. I stopped and got out of my car, tiny video camera in hand. Suddenly a Talib, black-robed and black-turbaned, rushed up and grabbed my camera. I thought he was going to break the camera, arrest me, shoot me. I thought to myself that I had survived five years of Taliban rule and the war, only to die now.

The man asked me who I was. I told him the truth and showed him my identity card. I thought that when he heard that I worked for a foreign news agency, I would be finished. But no, he apologized and handed back the camera. "I'm sorry, you work for a very famous and respectable news agency," he said. "I thought that maybe you were just someone looking for sensation, please go on with your work."

This was unprecedented, I knew the Taliban must be on the brink of defeat. That night, they fled the capital.

They will be remembered as a paradox—as young idealists who promised peace and an Islamic vision to a deeply Muslim people, and as severe puritans who presided over some of Afghanistan's darkest days.

A Taliban fighter pulls the lanyard to fire a Soviet-built 122-mm artillery piece north of the Afghan capital, November 24, 1996.

Dylan Martinez

Rebel soldiers, carrying arms and ammunition to the front line, walk under the protection of a mud wall during Taliban shelling in the battle for Kabul, August 5, 1997.

Jason Reed

Taliban security personnel wear their newly introduced traditional uniforms on a
road in Kabul, August 1, 2001.

Sayed Salahuddin

Sayed Salahuddin

Two Taliban fighters watch a soccer match in Kabul's sports stadium, June 26, 2001. The Taliban used the stadium to stage public executions.

Taliban fighters sit outside the American embassy before it was stormed by thousands
of angry demonstrators in Kabul, September 26, 2001.

Sayed Salahuddin

Adrees Latif

A Taliban fighter shouldering his weapon patrols the Afghan side of the Chaman border crossing, November 16, 2001.

Covered in her burqa, a beggar woman takes money from a car passenger in Kabul, June 30, 2001. Begging became prevalent after decades of war and years of harsh drought.

Sayed Salahuddin

Afghan land-mine victims watch as a fellow amputee walks on his artificial limb with
the aid of crutches at the International Committee of the Red Cross (ICRC)
Orthopedic Center in Mazar-i-Sharif, northern Afghanistan, August 11, 1997.

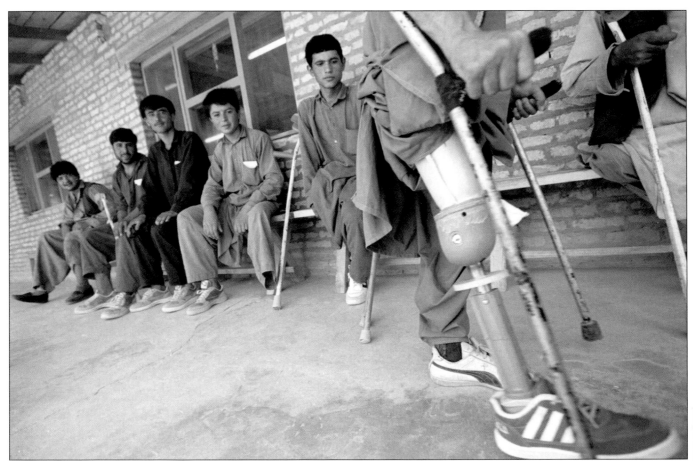

Jason Reed

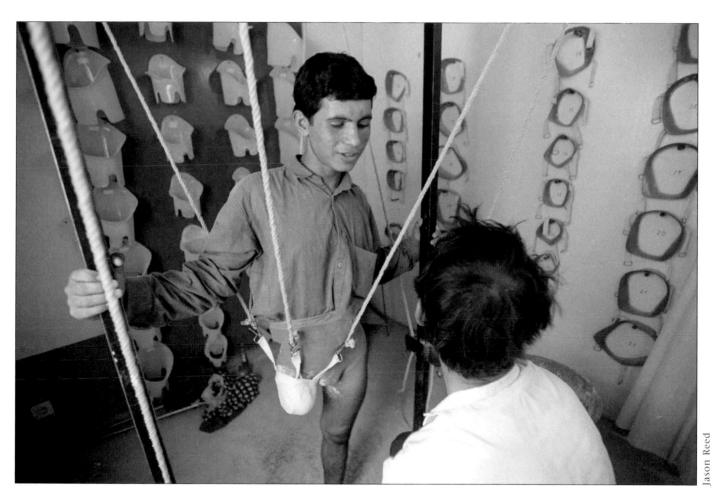

Jason Reed

A young Afghan land-mine victim is supported by ropes as a plaster cast of the remains of his leg is prepared at the ICRC Orthopedic Center in Mazar-i-Sharif, northern Afghanistan, August 11, 1997.

One of the giant Buddhas in the central province of Bamiyan seen from a distance, November 24, 1997. The Taliban destroyed the two statues because their strict interpretation of Islam forbade the depiction of false gods.

Sayed Salahuddin

A visitor walks past one of two ancient giant Buddhas in the central province of Bamiyan, December 18, 1997.

Muzammil Pasha

Taliban soldiers and visiting journalists stand in front of one of the destroyed Buddha statues in the central province of Bamiyan, March 26, 2001. The Taliban, despite international outcry, destroyed two giant Buddhas hewn into the limestone cliff more than 1,500 years ago.

Sayed Salahuddin

Two Afghan protesters try to remove the emblem of the American embassy in Kabul, September 26, 2001. Thousands of angry Afghans stormed the embassy in protest against U.S. plans to launch an attack on their country.

Sayed Salahuddin

Life Under the Taliban

Pawel Kopczynski

Taliban ambassador to Pakistan Mullah Abdul Salam Zaeef (right) gestures during a news conference in Islamabad as his translator looks on, October 19, 2001. In the initial days of the conflict, Zaeef became to the outside world the voice and face of the Taliban. After the downfall of the Islamic movement Pakistan handed him over to the American military.

The Enigma of
Osama bin Laden

Andrew Marshall

"I was thinking that the fire from the gas in the plane would melt the iron structure of the building and collapse the area where the plane hit and all the floors above it only," Osama bin Laden said of September 11. "This is all we had hoped for."

Curfew was in place. The Afghan capital was in darkness and streets were silent as three cars moved slowly down a road in the upscale Wazir Akbar Khan district. In front of them and along the roadside a number of scouts moved quietly on foot. A few minutes later a dozen landcruisers roared up and the scouts leapt into them. The whole convoy raced down the street and into the darkness. It was early 1998, and Osama bin Laden had paid a visit.

His cavalcade resembled that of a head of state. But he was no such thing. Or was he? He had been to call on Mullah Mohammad Rabbani, head of the council of ministers and deputy leader of the ruling Taliban. In Afghanistan, the status of this tall, thin, retiring Saudi-born millionaire, who changed the course of history in one of the world's poorest nations and in its richest, was always ambiguous. Afghanistan's Taliban rulers said he was their guest. Sometimes they said he was under their control. On occasion, they said he was missing. They never said what all the world suspected, that bin Laden may in fact have been running their country.

Osama bin Laden has left his fingerprints indelibly on history. A shy and often inarticulate man who spent much of his life in the shadows, hidden away in the world's most inaccessible places, he has become one of the world's most revered and most hated men.

His name and his bony, bearded face are recognized everywhere. As the world watched hijacked planes hurtle into the World Trade Center, watched the twin towers collapse, watched the Pentagon in flames and New York overshadowed by clouds of choking dust, the impact reverberated from the richest neighborhoods of the United States to the poorest and most desperate corners of Afghanistan.

To his admirers, bin Laden is the stuff of legend, a holy warrior who turned his back on the trappings of wealth for the austere and perilous life of a fighter. They lionize him as a man who took on the might of the world's most powerful nation in the name of religion. For the dispossessed and the angry in the Islamic world, bin Laden expressed their rage and directed it with such force at the country they blame for their suffering.

To those who vilify him, he is a mass murderer. He is a man so poisoned by hatred and extremism that he tries to justify the deaths of more than three thousand people, mostly civilians including women and children, in the name of religion. Leaning against cushions, gesturing with his long fingers, he could chuckle and grin at the devastation caused by the attacks on the nation that he so despised. U.S. President George W. Bush said he must be found—"dead or alive." He became the West's most-wanted man, with a $25 million price on his head, and uncounted billions spent on tracking him down.

The facts of his life have become entangled with myths, rumors, and propaganda.

At the heart of bin Laden's story, central to his journey toward the slaughter of September 11, 2001, stands the bloodied and beautiful country of Afghanistan. Afghanistan shaped him, transformed him, made him what he became. In return, bin Laden altered Afghanistan's destiny irrevocably.

Born in Riyadh in March 1957, he was the seventeenth son of construction magnate Mohammed bin Laden, who fathered more than 50 children. When Osama was born, his father was already rich. Over the next decade Mohammed became immensely wealthy renovating Islam's three holiest sites and grew ever closer to the Saudi royal family. In 1967 he was killed in a plane crash. His business empire, passed on to his sons, has prospered to this day and is worth billions of dollars.

One of the many mysteries of bin Laden's life is how this child of princely privilege was transformed into a Kalashnikov-carrying desert warrior.

Accounts of his childhood say he was brought up strictly according to the traditions of Wahhabi Islam and was tutored in theology from an early age. He has told interviewers that his was an austere start. He was expected to help work on roads his father's company was building.

Many of those trying to analyze his life and discover what drives him cite the death of his father as a turning point. Several commentators have remarked that throughout his life bin Laden has seemed to be searching for father figures. "Bin Laden's former associates describe him as deeply impressionable, always in the need for mentors—men who knew more about both Islam and the modern world than he did," said Pakistani journalist and Afghanistan expert Ahmed Rashid. He certainly surrounded himself with experienced military men or educated Islamic scholars as his military and strategic advisers. Peter Bergen, one of the few Western journalists to have met him, says bin Laden already showed an increasing interest in religion in his teenage years.

At 17, bin Laden married a Syrian relative, the first of his four wives. At King Abdul-Aziz University in Jeddah, where he studied for a degree in economics and public administration, he was profoundly influenced by leading figures in the Muslim brotherhood and their talk of fighting a jihad, or holy struggle, to build a pure Islamic state. And then—as it has so many times in history— remote Afghanistan moved to the center of world events. Soviet troops invaded in December 1979, outraging Muslims across the world.

Bin Laden had found a cause. At age 22, he travelled to Pakistan to meet Afghan leaders. Soon he was helping to raise money for the mujahideen from a house in the Pakistani town of Peshawar near the Khyber Pass. In the 1980s, taking advantage of his wealth and his construction expertise, he began making trips inside Afghanistan, bringing heavy equipment to build trenches, tunnels, roads, and bases for the anti-Soviet guerrillas. He helped the guerrillas to dig out the cave complexes from which they harried the Soviets. These were the rocky, earth-floored caves where many of his fighters, the Arab-Afghans as he called them, made their last stand against U.S. bombs in the final days of 2001.

The young millionaire was nicknamed the "Saudi Prince" by the mujahideen. Back home in Saudi Arabia, his admirers saw him as a hero, a child of privilege who renounced a life of luxury to take up the cause of jihad. With a fortune at his disposal, he set up a group called Khidmat, or Services, in Peshawar to pay for air tickets and accommodation and to deal with Pakistan paperwork for fighters en route to Afghanistan. To keep his operation running he established a network of couriers which still functions today, according to Rahimullah Yusufzai, a Pakistani reporter who has interviewed bin Laden. That network may have become bin Laden's way of keeping in touch with the outside world after 1997, when he suspected the U.S. security and intelligence agencies would be able to pinpoint his position if he used satellite phones.

His mocking messages to the outside world were delivered on videotapes. Those tapes have usually been delivered by hand to the offices of the Qatari satellite television station, al-Jazeera. The tapes reach al-Jazeera through a series of messengers, each with no knowledge of the next, to reduce the risk of tracing the tapes back to their maker.

It was in Peshawar that bin Laden founded his network, al Qaeda, which in Arabic means "the Base." But then the Soviet army withdrew from Afghanistan, the mujahideen took power, and the holy war was over. The victorious Afghan mujahideen recognized the debt they owed to the West. But for the "Afghan Arabs," such as bin Laden, gratitude toward the West was swiftly replaced by wrath. They felt that it was time for Muslims to fight their own war in defense of Islam and that Westerners had no place in it.

BBC journalist John Simpson, in his book *A Mad World, My Masters*, recalls an encounter in 1989 when he was in Afghanistan to make a documentary after the Soviet withdrawal. Filming near the eastern city of Jalalabad, later to become the heart of bin Laden's operations, Simpson and his team came across an imposing figure in white. "His robes were spotless," wrote Simpson, "and his beard sensational." The man harangued the mujahideen accompanying the BBC crew. An interpreter explained that the stranger was trying to persuade them to murder the foreigners. When the mujahideen refused, the tall stranger offered a nearby driver $500 to run down the journalists with his truck. Foiled again when the driver refused, the figure in white ran off. "We found him lying full length on a camp-bed, weeping and beating his fists on the pillow out of frustration at not being able to kill us. I almost felt like comforting him, but resisted, of course," Simpson said. Years later, Simpson saw a photograph of the mysterious man who had tried to kill him—it was bin Laden, who by now had achieved international notoriety.

The Afghan war turned bin Laden into a fighter. It was the Gulf War that turned him into an outlaw. His greatest test, the events that were to shift his ideology irreversibly toward war with America, lay just ahead. Returning to Saudi Arabia after the Soviets left Afghanistan, bin Laden began warning of the threat posed by Iraqi dictator Saddam Hussein. When Iraq invaded Kuwait, bin Laden thought he had found another holy struggle for al Qaeda's mujahideen—war against Saddam. The Saudis turned instead to the United States for help. Bin Laden was appalled. He has called it "the most shocking moment of my life." He found a new mission: to rid the Arabian Peninsula—the home of the sites most sacred to Islam, of Mecca and Medina—of the non-Muslims polluting the holy soil. This goal of wiping out Americans seems to have motivated him in his journey toward September 11.

People around the world were left asking the reason for this unprecedented attack. What was behind the deaths of more than 3,000 people? Bin Laden has never seemed to espouse a particularly coherent philosophy. His interviews and video statements are often distinguished more for their long, rambling, often dull tirades than for any focused objective. He has portrayed himself as a defender of Islam everywhere from Bosnia to East Timor, yet he has given little insight into the cause that drives him, beyond his hatred for the United States. Around the time of September 11, he added the Palestinian cause to his list of grievances against the West. Until then the burning anger that fuelled his bloody and meticulously planned attacks was the presence of U.S. troops on ground sacred to Muslims.

Bin Laden's increasingly virulent denunciations of the United States and the Saudi royal family became more and more of an embarrassment to the authorities, who tried to muzzle him and restrict his freedom of movement. In 1991 he left for a country that seemed more in line with his vision of a Muslim utopia—Sudan. It was ruled by radical Muslim Hassan al-Turabi, who, like bin Laden's later allies in the Taliban, aspired to create a pure Islamic state. Bin Laden invested in dozens of businesses in Sudan—everything from a bakery to a leather exporter to peanut farms—and built a major highway. He also gathered his al Qaeda followers around him, setting up training camps, preparing for war.

Financing also poured into military training camps in Yemen, and it was there, in 1992, that the first al Qaeda attack against U.S. military targets is believed to have taken place. In December, bombs exploded outside two hotels in Aden where U.S. military personnel were staying. An Australian tourist was killed.

Within a decade, al Qaeda would graduate from this initial single killing to the orchestrated horror of September 11. One of the few attacks for which bin Laden has publicly credited al Qaeda was the battle in Mogadishu, Somalia, between U.S. Army rangers and special forces and local warlords on October 3, 1993. Using lessons learned from the anti-Soviet campaign in Afghanistan, Somali fighters shot down two high-tech U.S. Black Hawk helicopters. Two more crash-landed at their base. In a savage firefight that raged for hours in Mogadishu, 18 Americans and hundreds of Somalis were killed.

By the mid-1990s, bin Laden had established several military camps in Sudan. In 1994 Saudi Arabia revoked his citizenship and froze his assets. Bin Laden was officially an outlaw.

Attacks proliferated. A truck bomb outside a joint U.S.-Saudi military installation in Riyadh killed five Americans and two Indians. Another truck bomb in Dhahran killed 19 U.S. servicemen and injured scores. Bin Laden said he admired and applauded the bombings but that al Qaeda was not involved—the same formula he has used when discussing almost all the attacks he is accused of masterminding. Analysts say those involved admired bin Laden and many almost certainly had al Qaeda training.

The United States had had enough. It put pressure on Sudan to expel the militant millionaire. That may have been a catastrophic mistake.

He was driven to take refuge in a land without law or government and to which U.S. influence did not extend. In May 1996 he flew into Jalalabad aboard a chartered jet, accompanied by dozens of al Qaeda allies and bodyguards as well as three wives and 13 children. Settling back into the mountain hideouts in eastern Afghanistan where he had fought the Soviets, bin Laden prepared a declaration of war. Writing on an Apple computer in August 1996, bin Laden issued his first formal call for a jihad against the United States. With a flourish he signed his declaration: "From the peaks of the Hindu Kush, Afghanistan."

Afghanistan was already falling into the grip of the Taliban. A month after bin Laden's declaration, the black-turbaned warriors of Mullah Mohammad Omar swept out of their southern stronghold of Kandahar to take control of the capital, Kabul. Bin Laden saw Mullah Omar as the personification of an ideal Muslim leader, a man determined to create the world's first pure Islamic state. The two men became friends, and bin Laden moved to Kandahar. A powerful alliance developed between the reclusive Taliban leader, who had lost an eye fighting the Soviets and who scolded his gardener for growing flowers rather than onions, and the soft-spoken millionaire, who loved horseback riding and surrounded himself with young zealots and theological tomes. It was an explosive combination.

Bin Laden may have been sick with kidney problems and in need of dialysis, but he was able to orchestrate the attacks that were to propel him from relative obscurity and onto front pages around the world. On August 7, 1998, two men drove a truck loaded with explosives to the gates of the U.S. embassy in Nairobi. The blast—at one of the busiest intersections of the city—killed 213 people, including 12 Americans. Nine minutes later a bomb exploded outside another U.S. embassy, in Dar es Salaam, Tanzania. It killed 11 Tanzanians. Days later scores of cruise missiles rained down on al Qaeda camps in eastern Afghanistan and on an alleged chemical weapons plant in Khartoum. "Our target was terror," said President Bill Clinton. "Our mission was clear—to strike at the network of radical groups affiliated with and funded by Osama bin Laden, perhaps the preeminent organizer and financier of international terrorism in the world today."

The U.S. strikes were a failure. Not only did they make no dent in al Qaeda, they outraged even Muslims opposed to bin Laden. "The attacks . . . had a major unintended consequence: they turned bin Laden from a marginal figure in the Muslim world into a global celebrity," Peter Bergen wrote in his book, *Holy War Inc.*

The terrorist attacks persisted. One in October 2000 bore bin Laden's fingerprints. Two men in a small boat laden with more than 500 pounds of explosives mounted a suicide attack on an American warship, the *U.S.S. Cole*, as it refuelled in Aden, Yemen. The explosion tore a gaping hole in the side of the warship and killed 17 U.S. sailors.

Shortly before the attack, a video of bin Laden was released in which he wore a Yemeni dagger. Around the same time he is said to have married his fourth wife—a 17-year-old Yemeni. That may have been no coincidence. His accusers say the dagger was bin Laden's signal that he was behind the coming attack on the *Cole*.

Less than a year later came the devastation of September 11. One of the most powerful symbols of America's might was reduced to rubble. A video found in Jalalabad after the rout of the Taliban shows him exultant, jubilant, boasting about the attacks that exceeded his expectations. "I was thinking that the fire from the gas in the plane would melt the iron structure of the building and collapse the area where the plane hit and all the floors above it only," he said in a video. "This is all we had hoped for."

This time the United States would not be content with firing a few cruise missiles at the mud-and-timber huts of Afghan training camps. Bin Laden had aroused the ire of the world's wealthiest nation, and it turned its full wrath on the militant and his Afghan hosts.

No more could the tall, gaunt Arab in flowing white robes gallop on horseback through the rugged Afghan countryside. He knew that after such a dramatic attack he would be hunted relentlessly—for as long as it took to capture him. Those who met him in the days and weeks after September 11 say he was ready to die. He was following in the tradition of the mujahideen who charged into battle against the Soviets hoping for martyrdom. Some even wept at their misfortune of having survived.

Bin Laden appeared to choose the same path as the hijackers who crashed their airliners into the World Trade Center. He was spoiling for a fight to the death. Hamid Mir, a Pakistani journalist who interviewed bin Laden inside Afghanistan in November 2001, said he almost revelled in the prospect. "Osama told me he would fight to the last drop of his blood," Mir said. "He did not seem to be somebody who loves life. He is somebody who loves death." He may have miscalculated in his alliance with the Taliban. Afghan fighters were not suicide bombers. These were men who preferred to fight another day. The nonchalance of the Taliban infuriated bin Laden's right-hand man, the Egyptian Ayman Zawahri, believed to be the brains behind al Qaeda. "They are just sitting playing chess and playing volleyball while we are getting bombed," Zawahri said in conversation with Mir just days before the Taliban collapsed.

Pounded from the air by withering U.S. strikes and cornered on the ground by the Afghan soldiers fighting the Taliban, thousands of al Qaeda were killed. Often they put up an astonishing fight. In the northern province of Kunduz, encircled al Qaeda soldiers withstood a bitter siege for more than a week against overwhelming odds. Some blew themselves up with their last grenades; others drowned themselves in the Oxus River rather than face capture. In a mud-walled fort near Mazar-i-Sharif, imprisoned al Qaeda fighters seized weapons and mounted a bloody uprising, holding out for days in its dungeons and passageways despite repeated ground assaults and waves of U.S. anti-personnel bombs. One of the rebels was a young American, John Walker Lindh, who had left small-town America and ended up fighting with al Qaeda, showing that even a U.S. citizen had fallen under bin Laden's spell.

In eastern Afghanistan, al Qaeda soldiers guarding bin Laden in the Tora Bora tunnel complex repeatedly refused to surrender even in the face of nightly bombing raids. Many were blown to bits by the force of the blast in their little caves. Bin Laden's voice was heard crackling over the radio waves, apparently directing his forces. Some said it was a previously recorded audio tape designed to mislead the Americans. As the U.S. military unleashed its awesome air strikes, officials in Washington said bin Laden might be trapped, might have slipped away, or might even have died in a dirt cave.

It is too early to declare the defeat of al Qaeda. Destroyed in Afghanistan, the network may still have enough operatives around the world to mount new attacks. The nightmare scenario of al Qaeda acquiring the nuclear and biological weapons they have sought for years still haunts the United States.

As for bin Laden, the myth may be as dangerous as the man. He inspires disgust among millions. And yet others regard him as a hero. In flowing robes and a camouflage jacket, a white turban wound around his head and holding a Kalashnikov assault rifle, this bearded figure has become an icon for the disenfranchised in the Islamic world. Osama is a popular name for newborn boys in several Muslim countries. Will these baby boys grow up sharing his hatred? Will a new generation carry on his fight? The war in Afghanistan has been won, but the battle for hearts and minds is still being waged.

Only when this battle has been won or lost can the final chapter of Osama bin Laden's life be written.

Wearing his trademark camouflage jacket and with a Kalashnikov rifle propped by his side, Osama bin Laden sits during an interview with a Pakistani journalist in an image supplied by the *Dawn* newspaper, November 10, 2001. The picture showed that bin Laden had survived a month of heavy American bombing.

Hamid Mir/Editor/*Ausaf Newspaper* for *Daily Dawn*

UBL: They were overjoyed when the first plane hit the building, so I said to them: be patient.

Defense Department Handout

In a chilling video clip released by the Pentagon, Osama bin Laden (left) smiles as he talks of the destruction caused by the September 11 attacks. Bin Laden showed prior knowledge that a second plane was heading for the World Trade Center, saying of his followers: "They were overjoyed when the first plane hit the building, so I said to them: be patient."

Guatemalans set fire to an effigy of Osama bin Laden at an annual devil-burning festival in Guatemala City, December 7, 2001. Guatemalans traditionally set fire to effigies of devils and piles of rubbish at street parties across the country to drive away evil spirits.

Jorge Silva

Jerry Lampen

A Pakistani boy clutches a toy AK-47 assault rifle at an anti-U.S. demonstration in Quetta, October 26, 2001. Pakistan's government supported the U.S.-led military operation in Afghanistan, but some Pakistanis openly showed support for Osama bin Laden.

A Bolivian girl displays a new table game, "War Against Terrorism," at a Christmas promotion in La Paz, December 17, 2001. The winning player is the first to find Osama bin Laden.

David Mercado

A Filipino vendor displays Osama bin Laden T-shirts at a Christmas sale at the mall of Zamboanga, in the southern Philippines, December 19, 2001.

Romeo Ranoco

Jeff Mitchell

It was just over a week after September 11 on a hot Dallas morning when I heard about a gun range offering targets of Osama bin Laden.

We all felt pretty numb in Texas, shell-shocked and subdued, being so far from what had happened. The gunshop owner had taped photocopies of bin Laden's face to the standard targets at the range so people could take a pop at him. Some shooters felt if they couldn't be in the military they could let off steam by firing their guns at bin Laden.

It was no joke; people were deadly serious. Texas is gun culture big time, it's a "right to carry" state, and this was an outlet, a way of making them feel better. While I was there a couple of guys came in with their own guns and ammunition; they'd heard about the targets. One of them was dead on, eight shots—all to the head.

Jeff Mitchell

The Unseen War

Jane Macartney

"Our Islamic state is the true Islamic system in the world and for this reason the enemies of our country look on us as a thorn in their eye and seek different excuses to finish it off," Mullah Omar said a week after the World Trade Center crashed to the ground. *"Osama bin Laden is one of these (excuses)."*

Packed into two four-wheel-drive pickups, armed to the teeth with Kalashnikov rifles and rocket-propelled grenades, the Taliban fighters were racing back to their hostel just before dawn. As they sped around a traffic circle in the city center, a huge explosion rocked the night. "I'm dying, I'm dying, I'm dying," a voice screamed, followed by silence. Prowling the skies high above, a U.S. jet had spotted the lone cars on a street emptied by the nighttime curfew and had struck with deadly accuracy. Unnerved, the Taliban authorities swiftly removed the wreckage and the bodies. No one learned how many had been killed. A few scraps of flesh and stains of blood on the street were the only signs left of the U.S. attack.

For those on the ground, the war seemed incomprehensible. The enemy was unseen in a war that began from the sky and was waged from the sky. For the thousands of occupants of the World Trade Center and the Pentagon, death came quickly out of a clear blue sky on a day that was to change the world. The Taliban, too, never really knew what had hit them. Even Hollywood would have scoffed at a fictional script in which airliners piloted by suicide hijackers ploughed into the twin New York skyscrapers that symbolized the might of the world's financial capital, sending them crashing to the ground. Who can forget the look of disbelief on the face of President George W. Bush as his chief of staff whispered the news into his ear?

The expression was instantly transmitted to countries around the world with one notable exception— Afghanistan, where television was banned. Not even Taliban supreme leader Mullah Mohammad Omar would have seen the searing images of the twin towers ablaze.

It was soon the turn of Afghans to be disbelieving as U.S.-led forces remorselessly went to work dismantling the rule of the Taliban. People in Afghanistan—civilians, Taliban, al Qaeda—never really understood what was happening when a wrathful United States unleashed the might of the world's most modern army on one of the poorest, most benighted states.

The U.S. military strategy defied conventional wisdom. This held that an air war could not be conducted against a country with no infrastructure, and that any foreign power that took on Afghanistan would retreat with its tail between its legs like the Soviets in 1989 and the British before them. But the United States succeeded with a bizarre combination of high-tech weapons and cowboy-style horsemen that had been never been seen before and may never be seen again.

The Afghan campaign came across as almost unreal. U.S. special forces dressed as Afghans worked on the ground with lasers to guide bombs to their targets; Taliban fighters switched sides at the drop of a hat; and above all, Bush's arch enemy, Saudi-born millionaire Osama bin Laden, remained a man of mystery, emerging only occasionally from his hideaways to taunt America with mocking videotapes.

Taliban leader Mullah Omar, an ethnic Pashtun village cleric born in 1959, a veteran who lost an eye in the war against Soviet occupation, had never traveled farther than Pakistan. He probably had no real concept of the destruction he would bring down on his people by refusing to hand over the tall, thin, bearded militant accused of orchestrating the September attacks. "Our Islamic state is the true Islamic system in the world and for this reason the enemies of our country look on us as a thorn in their eye and seek different excuses to finish it off," Omar said a week after the World Trade Center crashed to the ground. "Osama bin Laden is one of these (excuses)."

For the Taliban, as for bin Laden, a war against America was a struggle between Islam and the infidel. Bush was at pains to say this was not so and that his was a war on terrorism. When the Americans asked for bin Laden, Mullah Omar ignored them. When Pakistan sent in Islamic clerics and the head of their military Intelligence, which was credited with creating and nurturing Omar's movement, he offered them stewed lamb and pomegranates but not bin Laden. Omar said Islamic codes of conduct required him to give sanctuary to those who sought it, and he could not give up bin Laden without proof of his guilt. More than that, he was bound by the centuries-old unwritten code of honor of his Pashtun ancestors, which his people believe they must uphold even at the cost of their lives.

The Taliban warned the United States that the bodies of its soldiers would be dragged through Afghan streets, as they were in Mogadishu, Somalia, in 1993. "We grew up in war. Let the United States send its troops into Afghanistan. We will teach them a telling lesson," challenged Taliban fighter Khanzada, a rocket launcher slung over his left shoulder and a Kalashnikov rifle in his right hand, on the tenth day of the war.

But he and his comrades-in-arms had little idea what they were up against. Mullah Omar's footsoldiers were young men with a rudimentary religious education under orders from leaders imposing a 1,300-year-old imaginary Islamic utopia. The ban on television was part of that drive for purity. While it innoculated the country against what the Taliban saw as the decadence of Western civilization, it also meant that the militia had barely the faintest knowledge of the firepower that was to engulf them from the skies. They were to learn that rusting Soviet-era tanks could be no match for spy planes able to see a goat on a hillside and laser-guided missiles launched hundreds of miles away from submarines against people who have never seen the sea.

The attacks on September 11 were more deadly even than the Japanese raid on Pearl Harbor in 1941 that brought the United States into World War II. Americans recalled ·the words that Japan's Admiral Isoroku Yamamoto uttered at that time: "I fear we have awakened a sleeping giant and instilled in him a terrible resolve."

In planning its response to September 11, Washington had learned from Moscow's mistakes. It did not send in a massive army of occupation. Instead, its air force relentlessly ground down the Taliban supply lines and demoralized front-line troops with carpet bombing, while small numbers of elite special forces were deployed to coach and co-opt the Taliban's Afghan foes—the Northern Alliance grouping of mujahideen, or holy warriors.

"The Taliban depend on their military," said U.S. Rear Admiral John Stufflebeem. "Despite bravado about how they sent Soviet troops running, this is a different day." As they had done a decade earlier in the Gulf War against Iraq, the Americans prepared for the campaign carefully and patiently at sea and on the ground.

By the time the Americans had moved all their forces into place, nearly a month had elapsed since the attacks.

It was October 7 and the 9 p.m. curfew in Kabul had just begun. Twenty-five miles away to the north, on a hill just behind the Northern Alliance front lines, Reuters cameraman Sergei Karazy saw four bright flashes light up the night sky as the first cruise missiles struck the Afghan capital.

The missiles were to rain down for weeks in an unequal combat: the cost of those fired in the first two days alone almost equalled Afghanistan's entire $90 million budget for the year. Their targets were airfields, antiaircraft positions, the mud huts of al Qaeda training camps, military bases, tanks, field artillery, and a main residence of Mullah Omar in his power base in the southern city of Kandahar. Among the first victims were the 10-year-old son of Mullah Omar and his stepfather, killed when one of the deadly accurate bombs scored a bull's-eye on the reclusive cleric's house. As the days passed, the strikes intensified. From the ground, the Taliban opened fire at their unseen enemy with antiaircraft guns. Within days those guns had fallen silent, pulverized by U.S. bombs. Frustrated Taliban fighters fired their Kalashnikovs in vain toward the sound of jet fighters screaming a mile above their heads.

In Kabul, people lived in terror of the nightly attacks. In a city shattered by warfare, residents had never felt bombs of such force. "We are already in a big mess. What else does the world want from us? Drop one atom bomb and annihilate us all instead of killing us gradually," said one distraught resident, a neighbor of the victims of one of the first miss-hits of the war. Four mine clearers for a U.N.-sponsored nongovernmental organization were killed in their beds in a predawn raid by warplanes on a Kabul suburb. Rescue workers found one leg.

The Taliban said hundreds of civilians were killed in the air raids.

The Americans accused the Taliban of exaggerating the toll but said it was impossible to avoid civilian deaths altogether. They said the Taliban had brought the war upon themselves, but acknowledged that some of their bombs and missiles had hit the wrong targets.

A week into the bombing, Kabul resident Nazirullah watched in despair as a bulldozer tore at the rubble of his mud-baked home following a direct hit. The badly damaged bodies of his wife, sister, brother, sister-in-law, and mother were laid out in a row near the dusty ruins. "It's like doomsday for me," he said, gesturing in a daze toward the bodies, his hand missing several fingers—lost in fighting in earlier years in Afghanistan.

For the children of one of the world's most war-scarred capitals, the nightly raids heralded by the roar of planes overhead were especially traumatic. Sadeq was like any other five-year-old, inquisitive and talkative, spending his days exploring and playing in the street. As soon as night fell, he changed. The sound of an airplane turned him into a frozen statue. The noise of an explosion triggered a frenzy of shivering.

"The doctors have assured me that he will be all right," said his mother, sitting beside his hospital bed in Kabul. He had just been getting ready for bed when a bomb landed near his family's home. In the subsequent confusion Sadeq went into shock. "It was nighttime and we couldn't help him. The next day he had forgotten his name," said his mother, swathed from head to toe in a pale blue, pleated burqa. "We were forced to bring him to this hospital and now he laughs . . . but when the strike starts he shivers again and weeps." Later his family would take him home again, to wait and hope that no stray bomb would shatter his sleep. "We can't help him here in the darkness of the night," said one doctor. "We just hope that by sending him home he will be safe."

Taliban positions were scattered throughout the city among the homes of ordinary residents, and one bomb landed so close to a hospital that it shattered the windows at the back of the building. Two other bombs were targeted so accurately that they took out the transmitting room and the sitting room in the house of Qatari satellite television station al-Jazeera—the channel chosen by bin Laden to transmit his messages to the outside world. The reporters had left a day earlier. In a land with barely any telephones, where even messages to bin Laden are delivered by hand, no one really knows what the death toll was. The same goes for casualties among the Taliban and their allies in bin Laden's al Qaeda network.

"We are systematically pulling away at those legs underneath the stool that the Taliban leadership counts on to be able to exert their influence and power," Stufflebeem said on day 11 of the bombardment. The men who dropped the bombs spent hours in the sky. Many complained of sore behinds from being cramped in the cockpit seeking their targets—increasingly elusive as the war gathered pace. Then it was time to return to their bases on aircraft-carrier groups in the Gulf and the Indian Ocean for dinners of pizza on Fridays, occasional treats of Baskin-Robbins ice cream on the deck, and time out to email home. On the ground, their enemy was camped out in dusty trenches, their pockets filled with raisins that the Taliban leaders bought in bulk to keep their soldiers going in the field.

By early November the bombing had been going on for a month. Afghans started to wonder whether the Americans would ever defeat their enemy, whether the unseen bombs would ever stop, whether any targets remained to strike in a land of mountains and deserts. Armchair generals began to ask whether a war from the air could ever cow a people renowned for their courage. Even the U.S. president started to murmur about a long, drawn-out war and to warn of soldiers returning in body bags.

But few Americans were killed in combat, and limiting deaths was a goal of this war from the air. Secretly and silently, small numbers of U.S. special forces were advancing on the ground. The United States found eager allies in the Northern Alliance. The mujahideen groups that made up the motley alliance were hungry for revenge against the Taliban, who had thrown them out of Kabul five years earlier when their violent civil war, their brigandry, rape, and pillage, became too much for Afghans to bear.

Many wondered if the Tajik, Uzbek, and Hazara members of the Alliance could ever mount a viable offensive from the small pockets of the north into which they had been pinned by the mainly Pashtun Taliban. And the Alliance was leaderless. The greatest hero of the war against the Soviets, the hawk-nosed, dark-eyed veteran Ahmad Shah Masood, was gone. On September 9 the man known as the Lion of the Panjsher—after the steep-sided valley of his birth—invited two men he believed to be Arab television journalists into his office. They had waited 15 days for the interview. Masood's security guards searched the pair, checked their equipment, and brought them into the room. Before the interpretation of the first question was finished, one man had detonated explosives around his waist and the video camera blew up. The most-famed military strategist of the mujahideen and the worst enemy of the Taliban was mortally wounded. In what was surely no coincidence, two days later the suicide hijackers struck in New York and Washington. Masood had no clear successor from among the squabbling groups in the Alliance.

But one man seized the opportunity presented by the war. General Abdul Rashid Dostum is a hard-drinking, gruff-voiced ethnic Uzbek warlord. He had blown with the wind for more than a decade, deserting the Soviet government to join the mujahideen, only to be humiliated and vanquished in his power base in the northern city of Mazar-i-Sharif after one of his own commanders gave the keys of the city to the Taliban. Now he had established himself outside his former stronghold, a city famed for its blue-tiled mosque and its love for the game of buzkashi—an ancient, rough-and-ready version of polo in which dozens of men chase the carcass of a headless goat around the field.

The desert steppes around Mazar-i-Sharif are rugged and forbidding. Short of equipment, Dostum had to take to horseback. "We have witnessed the horse cavalry bounding . . . from spur to spur to attack Taliban strong points," said one of the U.S. special forces soldiers assigned to advise the warlord. The special forces called in strikes, and Dostum awaited his moment. It came sooner than even he had anticipated. By early November, one of the most devastating weapons in the American arsenal had been dropped on the Taliban front lines near Mazar-i-Sharif. It was the "Daisy Cutter," a 15,000-pound (6,800-kg) bomb the size of a Volkswagen Beetle that explodes in a fiery mix of air and fuel just a few meters above the ground. "We've been on the ground and it had the desired effect," said Air Force General Richard Myers, chairman of the U.S. military Joint Chiefs of Staff. Asked what effect was seen, he said "Dead al Qaeda." The Taliban never had the slightest inkling that weapons of such force existed. They began to waver.

The Taliban also had to endure carpet bombing from huge B-52 bombers. The Vietnam-era planes roared over Kabul in waves and swept unopposed over the Shomali plain north of the capital to dump their trademark sticks of bombs on the Taliban's World War I-style front-line trenches. The explosions threw up great walls of flame and columns of ash, and dust billowed hundreds of meters into the air. "These attacks are spot on," said Northern Alliance commander Rellozai, as he observed the string of explosions from his rooftop position in the front-line village of Rabat. Amid the Northern Alliance chuckles and smiles, some raised voices of caution. Rellozai, his walkie-talkie crackling constantly, opened his notebook to calculate the likely Taliban casualties after a month of bombing. He guessed that perhaps 500 Taliban had been killed. More softening up was needed, he believed, before the Alliance could be sure of victory.

Information about the enemy was scant. During much of the fighting, Northern Alliance forces and their Taliban opponents had swapped insults by radio. But these links were severed by the "Arab" volunteers deployed to stiffen the militia's ranks. These fearsome Chechen, Arab, Egyptian, and Pakistani fighters had no time for the taunts and jibes that had crackled over the airwaves.

The picture was clearer in Kabul. Doctors at the military hospitals on the edge of the city whispered that the Taliban death toll had soared, swelling to more than 400 in just a couple of days. Fighters driving to and from the front line were sitting ducks for the all-seeing Americans. The toll rose higher. The authorities put on a brave face, but their command and control ability had been destroyed, their front-line soldiers were dying. For the Americans, one of their biggest successes was the bomb that killed Mohammad Atef, an Egyptian, one of bin Laden's two top lieutenants and the suspected military mastermind of the September 11 attacks. "What kind of an army are these Americans?" Mullah Omar's driver, Qari Saheb, was quoted by *Newsweek* as saying. "It was amazing to see how they destroyed all our tanks."

In the north, the Taliban's morale was also crumbling. The bombing was of an intensity they had never imagined, called in by U.S. special forces and by Afghan spotters in the cities, who risked death to dial in by satellite telephone the latest sighting of Taliban or al Qaeda fighters.

The mainly Pashtun Taliban feared that ethnic Tajiks and Uzbeks in the north would rise up to take revenge for bloody massacres in Mazar-i-Sharif three years earlier.

Suddenly, the Taliban abandoned Mazar-i-Sharif and fled south as fast as their red Japanese pickups would carry them in the direction of Kandahar and Mullah Omar. On the evening of Friday, November 9, Dostum swept back into the dusty city. "While it looked like a ragtag procession, the morale in Mazar-i-Sharif was a triumphal procession," said one special forces soldier in his operation report. "Much waving, cheering and clapping even from the women."

Other towns in the north fell like dominoes and now all eyes were on the ultimate prize—Kabul.

The Northern Alliance was poised to attack, its aging tanks lined up in the vanguard, its soldiers dressed in ill-fitting, still-creased fatigues just out of their packing crates. Commander General Baba Jan advanced with his men over the rocket-pocked tarmac of Bagram air base and toward the Taliban front lines defending the capital. Overhead, U.S. bombers dived on the trenches, while at his side were more U.S. special forces—stern-faced men in jeans and sunglasses armed with M-16 assault rifles, scarves often tied over their faces to thwart identification. The advance turned into a virtual rout. The Northern Alliance took the two forward lines of Taliban trenches. The troops could scarcely believe that they now stood in positions at which

they had gazed from afar for five years. The Taliban could scarcely believe it either. Five years earlier, the Taliban had needed just a few days to seize Kabul from the mujahideen. When they relinquished the city, it was even quicker. They left within hours.

The leadership was the first to disappear. At dusk, the headquarters of the Taliban intelligence service was in darkness. A spotlight at the door, always lit from dark until dawn, had been switched off. The lights were also out at the house of the chief justice, and his guard had disappeared.

As night set in, tanks and armored personnel carriers rumbled out of town. Cars and battered pickups packed with Taliban, their belongings bundled in sheets, sped south on the main highway toward Kandahar. Residents did not dare to venture out until the curfew ended with dawn prayers.

Edging gingerly into the street, Reuters correspondent Sayed Salahuddin bumped into a soldier dressed in fatigues standing beside a pickup. A portrait of the Taliban's mortal enemy, the late Masood, was pasted inside the windscreen. "We have taken Kabul," shouted the jubilant fighter.

Kabul residents watched nervously. They remembered these men as looters and plunderers whose violent battle for power had cost the lives of 50,000 Kabulis. But barely a shot was fired that morning. Little boys spat at the bodies of seven Taliban sprawled, abandoned and bloodied, in a city park. The bodies of a couple of suspected Arabs—the most hated and feared fighters in the Taliban and al Qaeda armies—hung from trees where they had been shot in a desperate last stand far from home and without hope of escape. As the hours passed without reprisals and the bulk of the Northern Alliance troops poured into town, Kabul residents began to smile, and then to dance and to sing. Some hastened to shave their beards, others to play music. A new era had begun.

The end-game in the north was much messier. Several thousand Taliban and al Qaeda fighters trapped in and around the city of Kunduz finally surrendered after nearly two weeks of withering U.S. bombing and Northern Alliance artillery attacks.

They did not give up without a bloody postscript. Warlord Dostum herded about 500 of the Kunduz prisoners into a huge nineteenth century folly of a fort, Qala-i-Janghi, its 65-foot (20-meter) high walls and mud-baked crenellated ramparts dominating the northern Afghan steppe near Mazar-i-Sharif. Two American CIA agents—Johnny Micheal "Mike" Spann and a man known only as "Dave"— entered Dostum's bastion to interrogate the prisoners. The men were meant to have been searched and disarmed. But two grenades were thrown and the fighters fell upon Spann, who killed some of his attackers before becoming the first American to fall to hostile fire in the war. Dave and several journalists, including Nikolai Pavlov and Shavkhat Rakhmatulayev of Reuters, escaped the courtyard only to be pinned down for hours by a hail of bullets as the prisoners seized weapons from the fort's armory and made a desperate last stand.

U.S. jets were called in to bomb the sprawling fortress, but it took nearly a week to put down the uprising. In a war that was largely fought away from the cameras, television footage showed a Northern Alliance fighter using the corpse of a Taliban soldier as a rifle rest, bodies littering the ground around him. The revolt ended only when Dostum's men flooded the basements of the fortress. They expected to find a few survivors. In fact, 86 Taliban emerged, dazed and hungry. Between 300 and 400 of their comrades lay dead—along with dozens of Northern Alliance fighters— raising suspicions among human rights groups that excessive force had been used to crush the uprising.

The war was stuttering to a finish. But, this being Afghanistan, there was no conclusive denouement.

In Kandahar, the Taliban's last stronghold in the south, the militiamen just melted like mist into the hills and drifted back to their villages.

It was an unreal conclusion to an unreal war—a conflict without pitched battles, fought and won—like the Kosovo campaign—with air power. It saw the first-ever deployment of pilotless attack aircraft in pursuit of a quarry who, at the end, hid in caves.

U.S. military commanders basked in praise for a strategy well conceived and well executed. "I guess maybe searching for fleas on a dog is one way that I would think of it," Stufflebeem said. "If you see one and you focus on the one, you don't know how many others are getting away." Many of the conquered became fugitives, and many questions lingered that would take long to answer—one above all: how could it take the most modern army on earth so long to track down bin Laden, a man with a $25 million bounty on his head whom Bush said he wanted dead or alive?

Two Marine CH-46 helicopters bank as they prepare to land on board the *U.S.S. Peleliu*, an amphibious assault ship sailing in the northern Arabian Sea, November 20, 2001.

Jim Hollander

Jim Hollander

A Navy F-18 Hornet takes off from the aircraft carrier *U.S.S. Carl Vinson* in the Arabian Sea, November 12, 2001. In the foreground are flight deck handlers, and the steam is from a catapult which launched the plane.

A Navy crew works on a U.S. warplane as the sun sets over the flight deck of the aircraft carrier *U.S.S. Carl Vinson* somewhere in the Arabian Sea, October 31, 2001.

Jim Hollander

Navy ordnance handlers wheel laser-guided bombs on the flight deck of the aircraft carrier *U.S.S. Carl Vinson* in the Arabian Sea as they prepare F-14 Tomcat and F-18 Hornet jet fighters for strike missions, November 13, 2001.

Jim Hollander

The vapor trail of a B-52 bomber makes an arc in the sky above a multiple rocket launcher at the border of Kunduz province, November 23, 2001.

Gleb Garanich

A B-52 bomber leaves a vapor trail as it flies over the border of Kunduz province, the only province in northern Afghanistan which was still under Taliban control at the time, November 22, 2001.

Gleb Garanich

Anti-Taliban fighters watch explosions from U.S. bombings in the Tora Bora mountains in eastern Afghanistan, December 16, 2001. Bombers unleashed a withering assault which helped to dislodge Taliban and al Qaeda fighters from cave complexes there.

Erik de Castro

Sayed Salahuddin

Kabul residents look into a deep crater in a main road caused by a U.S. bomb, October 28, 2001.

Pakistani demonstrators burn a U.S. flag
and shout pro-Taliban slogans in front
of the Faysal Mosque after Friday
prayers in Islamabad,
September 28, 2001.

Pawel Kopczynski

A mob of pro-Taliban Afghan refugees runs toward members of the international press at the village of Yarro, near the Pakistani city of Quetta, as a convoy of 25 cars carrying journalists heads to the border, October 10, 2001. No injuries were suffered by members of the convoy, who immediately returned to the safety of their hotel in Quetta.

Jerry Lampen

Gleb Garanich

Northern Alliance soldiers return from a front-line position after a battle near the town of Charatoy in northern Afghanistan, October 10, 2001.

A Northern Alliance soldier runs during an exchange of fire on the front line near the town of Zarkama, October 15, 2001.

Gleb Garanich

Gleb Garanich

In the heat of battle, Northern Alliance soldiers fire from front-line positions near the town of Charatoy in northern Afghanistan, October 10, 2001.

A horse-drawn cart carrying civilians and Northern Alliance fighters stops at the side of a road to let by a speeding Northern Alliance T-62 tank on its way to a front-line position in Rabat, north of Kabul, November 10, 2001.

Yannis Behrakis

Yannis Behrakis

An Afghan woman in a traditional Burqa walks in the foreground as a Northern Alliance armored personnel carrier carrying fighters and flying the Afghan flag drives to a new position in the outskirts of Jabal-us-Seraj, November 4, 2001.

Yannis Behrakis

I started out at daybreak on November 13, the day after anti-Taliban forces backed by U.S. bombs made their long-awaited offensive and dislodged the Taliban from the front line north of Kabul. The Taliban had fled the city overnight, and I raced to photograph Northern Alliance forces who were massing at the "gates of Kabul," just outside the Afghan capital. The main highway was littered with the corpses of Taliban fighters. Northern Alliance forces had ground to a halt, waiting for their orders. I began taking photographs of a young dead Taliban fighter prostrate at the side of the road. Inquisitive Kabul residents were gathering around the body when I heard the rumble of a tank. I stood to the left of the body and made the picture as the Northern Alliance tank passed by. I had just seconds to shoot the frame from the right angle and get the right exposure to show the shadows of the curious. I had only one shot. It worked.

Yannis Behrakis

Northern Alliance fighters on a Soviet-era T-62 tank drive past a shell-pocked bread factory as they enter Kabul, November 13, 2001.

Yannis Behrakis

Yannis Behrakis

Victorious Northern Alliance fighters sing patriotic songs as they enter Kabul, November 13, 2001. Fearing reprisals, the United States had appealed to the fighters to stay out of the city, but they were greeted by residents with celebrations.

Jubilant Kabul residents join Northern
Alliance fighters entering the city after
the Taliban fled, November 13, 2001.
Reports from across the country
heralded a total collapse of Taliban rule.

Yannis Behrakis

Marines aboard the *U.S.S. Peleliu* assault ship relax against their full battle gear as they study a list of English words translated into Farsi, November 25, 2001. The list included phrases such as "Lie down on your stomach!", "We are Americans," and "We are here to help." Hours later, these Marines were the first to storm into Afghanistan in a heliborne assault to establish a forward base near Kandahar.

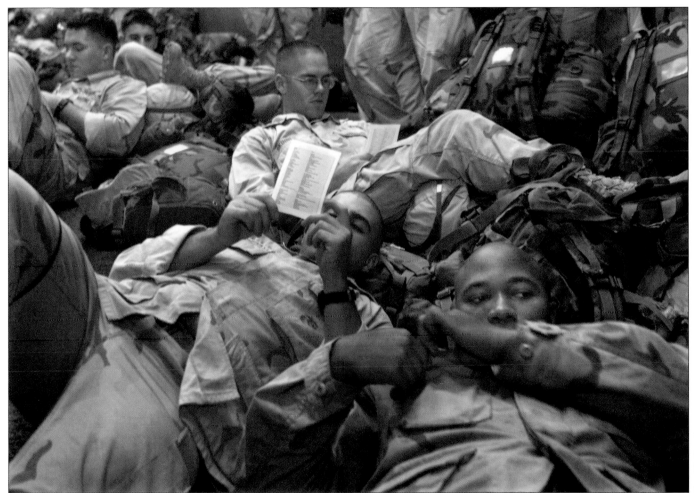

Jim Hollander

Marines from the 15th Marine
Expeditionary Unit raise two flags on a
bamboo pole at their base near
Kandahar, November 30, 2001. One was
a U.S. flag and another a flag given to
the Marines by New York City.

Jim Hollander

Passing makeshift cardboard signs, a
Marine carries empty sandbags to the
position of a light mortar company on
the front lines of the Marine base near
Kandahar, December 1, 2001. The signs
proclaim the name of the unit's base as
"Camp Justice."

WE THE PEOPLE OF THE UNITED STATES OF AMERICA.......
ARE GOING TO KICK YOUR ASS!!!
(THE NEW CONSTITUTION)

CAMP
JUSTICE
(FOR
AMERICA)

UNITED
STATES
OF
AMERICA
15,000 MILES

U.S.S.
PELELIU
600 MILES

AUSTRALIA
PERTH 6,000 MILES
SYDNEY 7,500 MILES

KANDAHAR
AFGHANISTAN
100 MILES

TALIBAN

Jim Hollander

127

A Marine writes a letter home to pass
the time in his front-line "fighting hole"
at the Marine base near Kandahar,
December 4, 2001.

Jim Hollander

Marine Cobra attack helicopters circle above larger CH-53 helicopters on the ground at the Marine base near Kandahar, December 4, 2001.

Jim Hollander

A speeding Marine Humvee throws up dust as it passes a group of light armored vehicles. It was setting off on a desert patrol from the Marine base near Kandahar, December 2, 2001.

Jim Hollander

Jim Hollander

A Marine ties down gear as he prepares his "Fast Attack Vehicle" for a desert reconnaissance patrol, December 3, 2001. The New York firefighters bumper sticker was sent out to the Marines.

A Marine Cobra attack helicopter flies past the setting sun on the perimeter of the Marine base in southern Afghanistan, December 3, 2001.

Jim Hollander

Rows of Northern Alliance soldiers rest on the front line at the border of Kunduz province, the only province in northern Afghanistan at that time still under Taliban control, November 24, 2001.

Gleb Garanich

An anti-Taliban fighter, covered with dust and carrying a rocket-propelled grenade launcher, rides on a truck to the Tora Bora mountains, December 16, 2001. Hundreds of al Qaeda fighters battled to the death there in a last stand in eastern Afghanistan.

Erik de Castro

Taliban prisoners stand in the yard of a jail at Khoja Bahawuddin in northern Afghanistan, guarded by Northern Alliance soldiers, October 18, 2001.

Gleb Garanich

An Arab prisoner is escorted by anti-Taliban fighters in Tora Bora, December 17, 2001. Followers of Osama bin Laden came under withering U.S. bombardment there.

Erik de Castro

A Nation of Refugees

David Fox

"To be a refugee is a terrible thing," said Sadako Ogata, who ran the United Nations refugee agency at the height of the Afghan crisis. "But a returning refugee is sometimes even more deserving of help and sympathy."

Something about the seas around Southeast Asia seems to attract shipping disasters—it could be the currents, it could be the typhoons. Perhaps it's just the law of averages, because with so many people traveling between so many islands, capsized ferries are bound to be tragically common.

So at first, the sinking of an Indonesian fishing boat off Christmas Island in August 2001 with 433 men, women, and children aboard appeared to be another unfortunate but almost routine event. But then the nationality of the passengers was revealed—they were almost all Afghans, thousands of miles from their landlocked home, trying to get to Australia.

Perhaps this should have come as no surprise. Since the 1970s Afghans have made up the world's biggest refugee population, desperately trying to get as far as possible from their war-ravaged land. In the process, they have tested the patience and hospitality of even the most hospitable countries. In the case of the shipwreck victims off Christmas Island, Australia refused to let them ashore. They spent ten days on the Norwegian freighter that saved them, languishing at sea, before Canberra paid the tiny Pacific territory of Nauru to take them in, offering to pay for their keep and providing millions of dollars in aid.

Weeks later, one of the few press visits allowed by authorities showed the Afghans living incongruously in seaside bungalows. The children kicked footballs along the powder-white beaches, the men smoked in huddles in the unfamiliar shade of coconut trees, and the women—unused to the luxuries of modern kitchens—prepared open fires over which to cook the family meal.

They were a long way from home.

World's Biggest Refugee Problem

About 12 years ago the United Nations estimated that more than six million Afghans were refugees—nearly a quarter of the entire population—and up to five million more were displaced within their own country.

Even as late as the end of 2001 more than two million Afghans lived in Pakistan, another 1.5 million in Iran, and hundreds of thousands in Russia and the independent central Asian republics of Kazakhstan, Kyrgyzstan, Tajikistan, Turkmenistan, and Uzbekistan.

Tens of thousands more had been granted asylum in Europe and North America, while nobody knows just how many affluent Afghans made up a less visible diaspora, blending into their new host societies by virtue of their wealth or political clout.

There is scarcely a country in the world where an Afghan hasn't shown up seeking asylum, leaving authorities shaking their heads in amazement and sometimes even admiration at their ingenuity and resourcefulness. From their Central Asian homes, Afghans have scattered across the four corners of the globe, applying for asylum in such far-flung places as Cuba, Haiti, Peru, New Zealand, Japan, Rwanda, South Africa, Taiwan, and Hong Kong. The most unlikely translocation was probably that attempted by one Afghan family who turned themselves in at a police station in Reykjavik and asked to become Icelandic citizens.

In Europe, the number of Afghans seeking asylum each year more than quadrupled in less than a decade from 8,500 in 1991 to nearly 35,000 in 2000. To each individual application, add another six people—the size of an average Afghan family.

More than 11,000 Afghans sought refuge in Germany in 2000 and 5,200 in Britain—up from 6,200 and 700, respectively, less than five years earlier. These huge increases continued even as authorities cracked down on illegal immigrants, making it more difficult for them to enter the country in the first place.

The overwhelming majority, however, settled just across Afghanistan's borders in scores of refugee camps dotted across the wild, inhospitable terrain. Over 3.2 million Afghans were living in Pakistan in 1990 and a further 2.9 million in Iran. The U.N. High Commissioner for Refugees says these figures are certainly on the conservative side, as they include only those registered in camps and not those who might be living and working among the general population.

The effect of such a mass migration of people can easily be seen in Afghanistan today. Thousands of towns, villages, and hamlets have been deserted for years. Irrigation systems have long succumbed to nature, vineyards grown wild and orchards unmanaged, so the only fruit they yield is small and sour. The brick walls of homes, schools, clinics, and mosques are crumbling back into the dusty earth from which they were made.

Trickle Becomes Flood

The first trickle of Afghan refugees was noticed in Pakistan in January 1980, just days after the Soviet Union invaded and installed its own government as the latest move in the international Cold War chess game.

The early arrivals were generally well-educated, middle-class professionals, fleeing because they represented the government that had just been overthrown or because their wealth or Western qualifications marked them out as the enemy.

Many of these first refugees were welcomed with open arms by neighbors keen to use their skills for a fraction of what it would cost to pay a Westerner with similar expertise. They became doctors in Pakistani hospitals and lecturers in Iranian universities. They used their entrepreneurial skills to open import-export businesses or trucking firms that attracted millions in transit taxes. They spent money and created jobs, but most of all they appeared to settle in well.

But what started as a trickle soon turned into a flood. The Soviet-controlled Afghan government found itself bogged down in a resistance war it tried for ten years to win before abandoning the attempt, just as the United States had done in Vietnam a decade earlier. The war was fought chiefly in the countryside, where bands of lightly armed mujahideen fighters ambushed convoys making their way from city to city before stealthily melting away into the landscape. The government extracted frightful revenge from villagers suspected of aiding the mujahideen, destroying crops or planting the countryside with so many land mines it became impossible to work. The cities, meanwhile, became bastions for those who backed the government. With nowhere else to go, millions of Afghans left the country.

Most headed for Pakistan. The colonial borders drawn up by Britain during the Victorian era had turned hundreds of thousands of people into Afghans or Indians (this was before the subcontinent's partition and the 1947 creation of Pakistan) merely by dint of where they happened to be living at the time. As many Pashtuns, Afghanistan's biggest ethnic group, live in Pakistan as live in Afghanistan. Families were scarcely inconvenienced by the red lines drawn on maps, and in many cases the divide actually suited them, creating a branch in each country—a useful setup for the smuggling activities that still dominate the Pakistan-Afghan border.

But the sheer number of refugees nearly swamped Pakistan. Huge camps were established that swiftly became breeding grounds for cholera, malaria, dysentery, and other epidemics. The effect on the local environment was catastrophic. Forests were hacked down in weeks to yield firewood for cooking, and crystal-clear rivers, fed by the snowmelt from the mountains that surround the area, were polluted in days.

The problems were the same on Afghanistan's western border, where hundreds of thousands of people poured into Iran—wreaking havoc on that country's environment, but also adding another element of chaos to a country caught in the grip of its own social change. As Iran wrestled with its Islamic Shia revolution, the Afghan refugees carried with them a rival Sunni orthodoxy that caused inevitable clashes—some of them tragic.

It was not always one-way traffic. After the Soviet withdrawal in 1989, millions of Afghans did return home, and the U.N. High Commissioner for Refugees actually said at one point that all refugees were expected to return by 1993. But they had not counted on Afghanistan's incredible capacity for conflict, and as the victorious mujahideen fell to squabbling among themselves over their prize, the exodus started anew.

The Taliban's triumph in 1996 prompted another brief turning of the tide, but eventually, for every Afghan who made the journey home, there was one ready to leave—weary of the harsh interpretation of the Koran that the country's new masters insisted on.

By the end of the 1990s, it seemed even nature was conspiring against Afghanistan. A four-year drought—the worst in living memory—drove hundreds of thousands to seek food across the border. An earthquake in the Hindu Kush mountains killed hundreds and made tens of thousands more homeless. Another exodus was the inevitable consequence.

Misery and Toil

Hussein Nazirahman is a typical Afghan refugee. He has lived for more than 20 years in Jallozai refugee camp near the Pakistani border town of Peshawar. He shares his three-roomed mud-brick house with his wife, five children, his father, a stepmother, a sister, and a sister-in-law. Of his children, three were born in Pakistan.

Hussein says he used to be a farmer, but it has been so long since he worked the land that he admits he has probably forgotten how. He still yearns, however, for the little plot of land he cultivated near Kabul until ordered off by Russian soldiers, who bulldozed his village after a convoy was ambushed nearby.

Hussein rises at five each morning, says his prayers, and then joins thousands of his fellow Jallozai residents on a usually fruitless quest for work. While Pakistan has been a tolerant host to millions of refugees, many Pakistanis have not hesitated to exploit the seemingly endless supply of cheap labor on their doorstep. If he is lucky, Hussein will get a few days work as a laborer on a building site, a porter in a market, or a cleaner. His temporary employer frequently sacks him before the day is done—throwing him out without paying him the pittance for his labors. If he complains to the authorities, he will be arrested. It is illegal for refugees to seek work.

Hussein's wife Fatima, meanwhile, will spend the day doing what refugees around the world seem cursed to do—stand in line for hours on end. There is a line for the water pump that more than 100 families must share. There is a line for the washing space at the ablution block. There is a line for bread rations and a line for soap. There is a line for clothing coupons for the children and a line for medicine for an aging parent. Virtually everything in Jallozai requires standing in a line—a mind-numbingly boring occupation that also pricks the pride of the fiercely proud Afghans.

The oldest son has a regular job in town. His fluent Urdu, picked up as a result of spending most of his life in Pakistan, makes him a more valuable commodity. He says all his earnings go back into the family coffers but admits—out of earshot of his father—that he keeps some back for himself. He is tired of the refugee life and is thinking of trying to find a Pakistani bride and possibly even applying for citizenship. The nest egg he is salting away will help him escape the shackles of extended family life.

The eldest daughter works in a carpet factory—her nimble fingers shaping the intricate patterns that make up an Afghan carpet. She is 16 now and due to be married shortly to a second cousin—one she has never met. She has no choice in the matter. Her marriage will earn the family around $100 in gifts and dowry.

The three youngest children attend one of the many schools that have sprouted in Jallozai camp—refugee schools run by refugee teachers with refugee curriculums.

Hussein's father, near-blind with cataracts in both eyes, spends his days at a refugee mosque, listening to a refugee cleric and reminiscing about the good old days with his fellow refugee pensioners.

On the surface, Jallozai is a slice of Afghanistan recreated in Pakistan, but the pressure of tens of thousands of people living on top of each other has inevitably taken its toll on the delicate web that makes up Afghan society.

Rape, almost unheard of in Afghanistan, is more common in refugee camps than elsewhere in Pakistan. Domestic violence is higher in the camps than outside, while theft and assault—hardly commonplace in either Pakistan or Afghanistan—are reported more often in refugee communities. Generations of subtle cultural tradition are being lost with the boundaries of the refugee camps—although not all of this tradition will be missed, according to some. Women, for example, have had to be given greater freedom in the refugee camps merely to keep families together.

The camps have also become breeding grounds for the type of Islamic fundamentalism that shocked the world on September 11.

Camp Economies

Chances are that if you buy one of Afghanistan's famous rugs or carpets anywhere in the world today, it was made in Pakistan. Certainly it was designed in Afghanistan, probably woven using Afghan wools and dyes, and almost certainly it was made by Afghans, but it will probably have been made in Pakistan, in an Afghan refugee camp.

By the late 1990s so little was left of Afghanistan's infrastructure that the country was manufacturing almost nothing. Pakistan and Iran provided better-paying outlets for the agricultural produce that escaped the drought, but nothing made in the country was worth exporting—apart from one nefarious product that the rest of the world said it would rather do without, opium.

The refugee camps of Pakistan provided the perfect hiding place for the scores of laboratories that turned Afghanistan's opium poppies into the substance the world's drug addicts injected into their veins. The United Nations at one point estimated that 95 percent of Europe's and 90 percent of the world's heroin originated from Afghanistan, and most of it hit the streets of the Western world via an Afghan refugee camp. Some refugees actually returned home every planting season to grow their poppies—each successive Afghan regime allowing the crop because of the "tax" it yielded for the state's coffers. If they were not actually growing poppies, Afghan refugees were involved in smuggling the raw opium across the border to be refined in Pakistan. Many were also used as couriers for the product, trafficking heroin abroad for the chance of a ticket out, even if the risk was life imprisonment or worse, depending on where they were caught.

While most Afghans followed the drug-trade mantra of "deal, don't dabble," thousands did succumb to the escape from their miserable lives that heroin offered and became addicts themselves. Dozens of addicts lie stoned out of their minds in sordid alleys of Jallozai camp.

Success in a New Life

Afghans who have made the transition from refugee to bona fide citizen of another country have usually quickly assimilated themselves into their new lives, their only handicap being language.

They found no job too humble to accept, filling in as cleaners, street sweepers, unskilled laborers, and farm workers in countries where the established citizenry would rather live on social security than do menial work. In most cases, the generation that made the break from the homeland also made enormous sacrifices to ensure an easier life for the next. The aim was to get the oldest child well educated and employed so that he or she could contribute to the family coffers.

There have been exceptions, and European jails have a fair-sized population of Afghans imprisoned for involvement in activities ranging from drugs to murder, but the new immigrants have generally tried hard to improve their lives, sparing their children nothing in a bid to better the family fortunes.

Afghan refugees have become musicians and artists, professional athletes and law enforcement officers, computer experts and scientists—their skills and talent boosting the wealth of their new nations as much as they deprived their homeland of their valuable human assets.

That brain drain is obvious in Kabul. Of 210 people from the Kabul University class of 1993, only one graduate remains in the country. The rest have left for greener pastures—most to Pakistan, but many also to the United States or Europe. The remaining graduate is still in contact with many of his classmates. They don't intend to return, he says.

Some of Afghanistan's most famous sons have abandoned their homes in despair at the country's seemingly endless woes. Abdul Haq, one of the mujahideen struggle's best-known commanders, finally wearied of Afghanistan in 1994 and settled in Dubai, where he took United Arab Emirates citizenship and became a successful businessman.

In the dying days of Taliban rule at the end of 2001 he returned once more to Afghanistan, aiming to rally supporters behind the effort to unseat the religious zealots. Two days after his return he was captured and accused of spying for the United States. His new-found optimism ended in front of a firing squad.

The Road Home

With the international community probably more optimistic now about Afghanistan's future than at any time in the last three decades, the United Nations and nongovernmental aid agencies are also hopeful that they will finally be able to solve the refugee problem.

Afghans, however, are cautious people, and years of disappointments have taught them to be wary of false dawns and new eras of peace and prosperity. Rather than returning in droves after the overthrow of the Taliban, they have still made a net exodus from the country. The United Nations has no plans to start persuading Afghans to return until spring 2002, arguing that the country simply could not cope with the sudden arrival of millions of its sons and daughters.

If and when the migration home begins, it is likely to cause joy and bitterness in equal proportions. Families will be reunited, but old enmity will also be renewed. Thousands of Afghans will find that, in their absence, strangers have moved onto their land or into their homes. New figures of influence have emerged in rural communities, and returning elders will find that their gray beards count for nothing with those who stayed behind.

"To be a refugee is a terrible thing," said Sadako Ogata, who ran the United Nations refugee agency at the height of the Afghan crisis. "But a returning refugee is sometimes even more deserving of help and sympathy."

Damir Sagolj

I took this photograph of children framed by a window in the former Soviet embassy. The walls, pockmarked by bullets, bore testimony to decades of war.

A sad and dangerous place, the sprawling rundown compound with tall walls and no running water was home to 15,000 refugees, mostly women and children. Angry mobs of the dispossessed could swiftly turn on a photographer. Some colleagues were attacked and stoned by a mob. The media were accused of wanting to get to the women's section, which was patrolled by armed guards, to photograph the widows.

Once in the compound I decided to spend some time in the bakery, run by an aid agency, to see what images emerged. My "escort" left me alone for a few precious moments. During that time I snatched this picture of curious children staring at the outsider.

Damir Sagolj

An Afghan boy gnaws on a bone in a refugee camp near the town of Hojabohhaudin
in northern Afghanistan, October 8, 2001.

Gleb Garanich

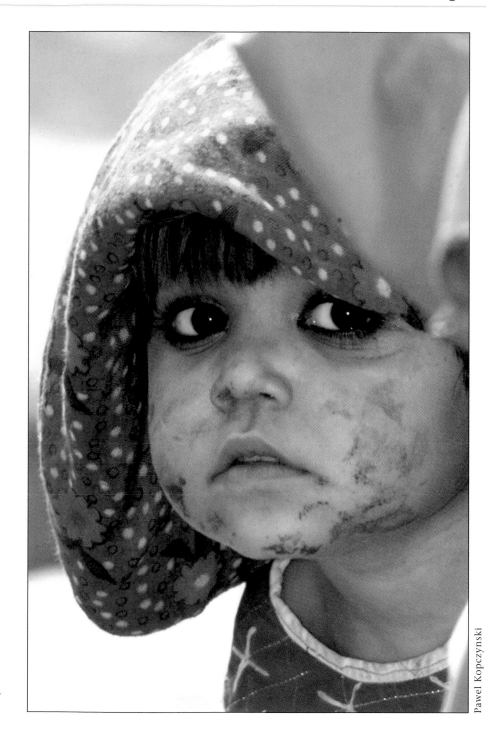

Shakria, a two-year-old Afghan girl, peeks at the village set up for Afghan refugees on the outskirts of Islamabad, October 2, 2001. The United Nations' top humanitarian crisis coordinator urged Pakistan to open its borders to hundreds of thousands of Afghans trying to flee hunger and a possible U.S. attack on the ruling Taliban.

Pawel Kopczynski

Pakistani military personnel check for identification as Afghans wait at the Chaman
border crossing, northwest of Quetta, November 26, 2001.

Adrees Latif

Jerry Lampen

Afghan refugee Abdul Hadi, 50 (right), and his 45-year-old cousin Hayat Khan talk about their homeland at a refugee house in Quetta after arriving from Kandahar, October 23, 2001. Abdul spent six days travelling to the Balochistan capital Quetta, near the Chaman border with Afghanistan.

An Afghan refugee walks into the Pakistani border town of Chaman with her belongings, November 29, 2001.

Adrees Latif

Afghan refugee Permina, 7, sits near her father Taj Mohammad (right) and brother Sat Mohammad, 11, in a Quetta hospital, November 8, 2001. According to their father, Permina and Sat were both injured by shrapnel during U.S.-led air strikes near the southern Afghan city of Kandahar.

Adrees Latif

An Afghan refugee receives polio drops from a Pakistani nurse at the Shamshatu
refugee camp near Peshawar, November 6, 2001.

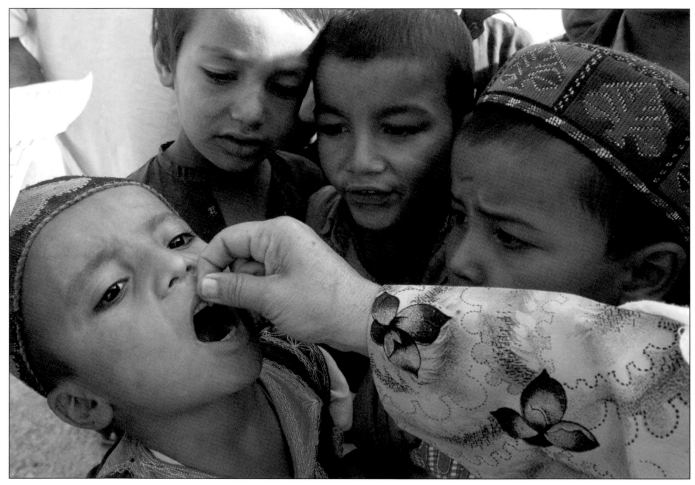

Pawel Kopczynski

Jerry Lampen

An Afghan refugee boy looks on as an older Afghan man counts his worry beads in their refugee camp at Boughri, close to the Pakistan-Afghan border, October 21, 2001.

An Afghan refugee girl in the Kili Faizu UNHCR Camp in Chaman, Pakistan, reacts
after spotting a jet in the sky, November 10, 2001.

Adrees Latif

Pawel Kopczynski

Seida, a six-year-old Afghan girl, swings on a rope at a village set up for refugees on the outskirts of Islamabad, October 6, 2001.

An injured Afghan refugee, 32-year-old Sada Bibi, looks at a young boy as she lies in a bed in a Quetta hospital, October 26, 2001. According to her brother, Sada was wounded in her village of Bohari, just outside the Taliban stronghold of Kandahar, during heavy U.S. bombing. In the attack, Sada lost five of her daughters, two sons, her husband, and two other relatives, her brother said.

Jerry Lampen

Rabia, a 25-year-old Afghan refugee, holds her daughter Snawba in Islamabad, October 4, 2001.

Pawel Kopczynski

An Afghan refugee begs while her children sleep on a roadside in the western Pakistani city of Peshawar, September 24, 2001.

Azizullah Haidari

A doctor weighs a child at a makeshift clinic in Shamshatu, southeast of Peshawar, February 17, 2001.

Azizullah Haidari

A severely malnourished Afghan child, Gul Baz, 2, is comforted by his father in a hospital in Peshawar, September 27, 2001. Baz weighed the same as a normal five-month-old baby.

David Loh

Jerry Lampen

Two Afghan children at their mud home in the Saranan refugee camp in Pakistan, October 4, 2001.

Anjer Mohammad sits next to his belongings in the Kili Faizu UNHCR Camp for
Afghan refugees near the Pakistan border town of Chaman, November 10, 2001.
Mohammad, who has 14 children and three wives, was about to be relocated
to another camp.

Adrees Latif

Adrees Latif

Afghan refugee boy Ramut Ullah collects water from a natural stream for his family in a UNHCR camp near the Pakistan-Afghan border town of Chaman, November 5, 2001. Many refugees struggled to find drinking water in the drought-stricken area.

An Afghan refugee prays near the Pakistan-Afghan border around Chaman,
October 21, 2001.

Jerry Lampen

Pawel Kopczynski

An Afghan refugee family sits on the steps of the United Nations High Commissioner for Refugees offices in Islamabad, October 4, 2001.

Displaced Afghan civilians return home by truck on the main highway north of Kabul, November 16, 2001. Vehicles packed with civilians and their belongings started returning to Kabul after the Northern Alliance troops pushed Taliban forces to the south.

Yannis Behrakis

Behind the Burqa

Rosalind Russell

"Without prompting, the two women pulled their veils back over their heads. Seeing my shock, they both began to giggle. I don't know what I expected, but it was not this: two teenaged girls, with red lipstick and matching nail polish, one in a denim jacket and the other in a red sweater with a white satin love-heart sewn on the front. I had been in Afghanistan for three weeks. These were the first women's faces I had seen."

Rosalind Russell

On my second day in Kabul I told my translator Naim that I wanted to meet some women. "And talk to them?" he asked. He seemed unsure. He had found field commanders, mujahideen veterans, and politicians without a problem, but this was a far more sensitive issue. After some thought he drove me to a residential district in the north of the city where Soviet-era four- and five-story apartment blocks lined potholed streets. Along one street were market stalls selling vegetables, dried fruit, and spices, busy with the faceless shapes of women, shrouded in their blue burqas. We slowed down by two of the ghostlike shapes and Naim leaned out of the window to talk to their escort, a young man in jeans and a leather jacket. The women would talk to us, the man said, but not there. He would drive them to a quiet rendezvous about half a mile away.

We drove on and parked away from the crowds. Soon a white Toyota sedan drew up behind us, the male escort in the driver's seat and the two women in the back. I climbed in and knelt on the passenger seat facing backward with Naim perched beside me. Without prompting, the two women pulled their veils back over their heads.

Seeing my shock, they both began to giggle. I don't know what I expected, but it was not this: two teenaged girls, with red lipstick and matching nail polish, one in a denim jacket and the other in a red sweater with a white satin love-heart sewn on the front. I had been in Afghanistan for three weeks. These were the first women's faces I had seen.

Roya was 18 years old and her cousin Najia was 15. Both had been schoolgirls when the Taliban took over in 1996, and their education was brought to an abrupt halt. Under the Taliban's strict interpretation of Islam, women were not allowed to work or study. They could only leave the house covered by the all-concealing burqa and accompanied by a close male relative or "mahram"—a husband, father, or brother. Women were forbidden from raising their voices or laughing in public, or wearing makeup or shoes with heels that clicked.

Taliban vice squads enforced the rules with vigor. If caught inappropriately dressed or without a proper escort, women were routinely beaten and often accused of more serious crimes such as adultery and prostitution. Married women would be stoned to death on such charges; single women could expect a public lashing.

For Roya and Najia, life under the Taliban meant one thing above all: boredom. In Afghanistan's traditional Muslim society they had never expected their teen years to be filled with boyfriends, discos, or illicit alcohol. But as middle-class girls they did at least expect to study with the hope of going on to university, to meet their friends, and to play music at birthday parties. Roya wanted to be a doctor or a journalist. "I was a good student, I always worked hard and got good grades," she said. "If it wasn't for the Taliban, I would be at university by now. But all this time I have been sitting inside the house, doing my sewing. It was boring. Sometimes we had nothing to say."

It was November 14, 2001, barely 24 hours after the Taliban had fled Kabul and Northern Alliance troops had moved in. The initial excitement had died down and there was a sense of uncertainty about what would happen next. It was no longer mandatory for women to wear their burqas, and some had dared to raise their veils, revealing shy and often beautiful faces for the first time in five years. But most stayed covered up. The Northern Alliance forces themselves had a poor track record of treatment of women when they held power in Kabul before the Taliban. Mujahideen soldiers were accused of raping women and girls and of using sexual assault as a means of intimidating the population. "We'll keep on wearing them until things settle down," said Roya. "We want to get rid of them, but we have to be careful."

The burqa is a garment that covers women from head to toe, the only window to the outside world a crocheted grille across the eyes. It can be white or gray, but blue is currently in vogue in Afghanistan. Inside it is dark and stifling, the wearer can hardly see more than a few steps ahead, and peripheral vision is completely blocked. Women bump into things, fall over, and even get knocked down by cars they cannot see coming. The obligation to wear the burqa was a severe financial hardship for poorer women, its cost equivalent to several months' salary. Sometimes women would share one garment, waiting several days for their turn and the opportunity to venture outdoors.

But the burqa was not an invention of the Taliban. In the cities, its strict enforcement came as a blow to middle-class, educated women. In rural areas, however, social convention ensured it was worn long before the Taliban took power. Women are considered as jewels to be seen only by their husbands and family. Without the burqa, they are regarded as immodest and unfit for marriage. In the patches of countryside held by the Northern Alliance during Taliban rule, women remained invisible and forgotten beneath the veil.

Women's groups in Afghanistan have criticized the West's obsession with the burqa and its removal; they argue that education and the right to work and participate in politics are the real issues that will emancipate Afghan women. According to the Revolutionary Association of the Women of Afghanistan, RAWA, a 25-year-old women's rights group, the end of the mandatory burqa is "in no way an indication of women's rights and liberties in Afghanistan."

Leyla, a 19-year-old living in a poor area of Kabul, put her finger on the real problem. After her school was closed by the Taliban, she ran a secret beauty salon, earning small amounts of cash for her hard-up family until religious police from the Ministry of Promotion of Virtue and Prevention of Vice raided her back-room parlor and confiscated makeup, mirrors, and a precious hairdryer. Now her business is up and running again, pulling in more and more clients as women warm to their new freedoms. But Leyla knows she must go back to school. "I know if I

study I could do something even better," she said. "I am 19, but I have the education of a child."

Girls younger than Leyla have no education at all unless they were taught in secret. Afghanistan's interim government has promised it will not discriminate between girls and boys in education, and already in Kabul, Kandahar, Mazar-i-Sharif, and other newly liberated cities girls' schools have reopened. Women teachers, who filled more than 60 percent of teaching posts before the Taliban, are coming back to teach both girls and boys in segregated classes.

But the schools that do exist are making do with very little—many have no desks, chairs, notebooks, pens, or chalk for the blackboard. Some were used by the Taliban as barracks or even for ammunition storage. In many areas of the countryside schools do not exist at all. The United Nations children's fund (UNICEF) estimates that just 16 percent of female adults in Afghanistan can read or write, compared to 46 percent of males. Other organizations such as RAWA say the figure is much lower—the result not just of Taliban policy but also of a rural social tradition that has never placed much value on the education of women.

Afghanistan's transitional government led by Hamid Karzai includes two women, both forthright advocates of women's rights, who have vowed to tackle the discrimination faced by Afghan women. Sima Samar, a 45-year-old medical doctor, was named as one of five deputy prime ministers—the highest office to be filled by a woman in Afghanistan—and given the portfolio of women's affairs. Samar has lived in exile in Pakistan since 1983, working as a doctor and running food relief programs for Afghan refugees, as well as establishing several schools, hospitals, and health clinics in Afghanistan as head of a nongovernmental organization. She has publicly condemned the compulsory burqa on the grounds that by reducing women's exposure to sunlight and consequently their vitamin D intake it aggravates common diseases such as osteomalacia, which softens the bones.

"My hope and my aim and my vision is that women's rights should be counted as human rights," Samar said after her appointment at a U.N.-sponsored meeting in Bonn. "Access to education, freedom of speech, freedom of working outside the house, freedom of choosing the way we are wearing the clothes, freedom of choosing their profession, access to health care, these are all basic human rights."

Samar's female colleague in cabinet is 62-year-old Suhaila Seddiqi, who was appointed health minister. A military surgeon with 38 years of service in the army medical corps, she was made a general in the early 1990s, the only Afghan woman in modern times to hold the rank. Seddiqi has seen regimes come and go, even surviving the Taliban, who at first fired her as the head of a 400-bed military hospital in Kabul, then asked her back to run the women's section. Seddiqi operated under her own rules. Known throughout Afghanistan as simply "the General," she eschewed the veil and lived alone with her sister—infringements of the law which the Taliban, whose wives and daughters she treated, chose to ignore.

Seddiqi trained as a doctor in the 1960s, one of the times of relative freedom for women which came and went during the twentieth century. In the 1920s, King Amanullah first moved toward the liberation of women. At a Loya Jirga, a meeting of the leaders of the country's ethnic groups, he condemned the mistreatment of women and requested that the queen lift her veil before the assembly. He introduced reforms permitting women to go without the burqa and opened several coeducational schools. But his liberated views alienated religious and tribal leaders and eventually cost him the throne.

Prime Minister Mohammad Daoud tried again in 1959 when he, his ministers, members of the royal family, and high-ranking army officers appeared at Independence Day celebrations with their wives and daughters unveiled, which again prompted a conservative backlash. Undeterred, in 1964 King Zahir Shah invited women to sit on the committee which drafted a liberal constitution guaranteeing equality for men and women.

The constitution was seen as a watershed for women's rights. The following year saw the appointment of Afghanistan's first woman minister, and in the cities women worked as doctors, teachers, and entrepreneurs. The Soviet-backed communist government that came to power in 1978 moved to prohibit traditional practices deemed feudal in nature—including the "bride price" through which the husband's family would purchase a chosen woman. By 1980 Afghanistan had seven women members of parliament. But two decades later, Afghan women are fighting prejudice and discrimination all over again.

At the Malalai Maternity Hospital in Kabul, Dr. Fahima Sekandari is called into the director's office. In a white coat and headscarf she sits on the edge of the couch, looking meekly at the floor. "She can't speak English but I can translate for you," said the director Mohammed Hashim Alokzai. "What would you like to ask?" We conducted a short interview. The director answered most of the questions himself. "She likes working here very much. . . . We had no problems under the Taliban except for a lack of funds. . . . She doesn't know the maternal mortality rate; we don't have such information." I asked if I could see the maternity wards and Alokzai agreed. "Of course I cannot go in myself, but she will take you."

We walked down the steps to a courtyard where dozens of fathers-to-be stood or squatted against the concrete walls waiting for news from inside the hospital. Once behind the heavy gray blanket that marked the no-go area for men, Dr. Sekandari bent over in peels of laughter, grabbing my arm. "Of course I can speak English!" she said. "He knows nothing about me."

Dr. Sekandari, a 42-year-old mother with glossy black hair, was a gynecologist with 14 years experience. Unlike most of her female friends, she kept her job under the Taliban along with other specialists in women's health care. Sixty doctors and 50 midwives worked at Malalai, Kabul's main maternity hospital where around 80 to 100 babies were delivered every 24 hours. The hospital was clean with a warm, professional atmosphere. Salaries had not been paid during the last few months of Taliban rule, and Dr. Sekandari said they lacked medicines, especially anesthetics for Cesarean sections. But compared to other hospitals in Afghanistan it was fairly well equipped and even had 10 incubators. It treated the lucky few; most women give birth at home and the World Health Organization estimates 45 Afghan women die every day due to pregnancy-related complications.

"Put these on and I'll take you into the delivery room," she said, handing me a white plastic cap, apron, and plastic covers for my shoes. Inside, a 10-minute-old baby boy had been weighed and was being wrapped tightly in white cloth. His mother lay exhausted and half-smiling on a delivery bed. The winter sun gleamed through a frosted glass window. This was a sanctuary the Taliban never touched. "No men are allowed in here," said Dr. Sekandari. "So we know it is a safe place."

Sadly, the security of the delivery room at Malalai hospital is far from the reality of most women's lives in Afghanistan.

During two decades of warfare in Afghanistan there have been few safe havens for women. They have rarely participated on the battleground but few have escaped violence. From whippings by Taliban militia for revealing an ankle, to the destruction of entire neighborhoods in fighting, women have carried the heaviest burden.

During the war of resistance that followed the Soviet invasion of 1979, millions of people left their homes and fled across the border to Pakistan and Iran or to relatives and camps inside the country. Civilians who remained in the firing line, including women and children, were targeted by Soviet and Afghan government troops in reprisal for what was seen as their support for mujahideen resistance fighters. The Soviets withdrew in 1989, but within a few years rival mujahideen factions had turned their guns on each other. Under the nominal rule of President Burhannudin Rabbani from 1992 to 1996 the capital descended into full-scale civil war, with indiscriminate shelling of civilian areas.

There are more than 30,000 widows in Kabul as a result of war. Often destitute, they had one important lifeline, the so-called "widow's bakeries" funded by international aid agencies. The bakeries were run by Afghan women and sold bread at subsidized prices to the city's widows. For thousands it was their only means of survival. The Taliban had allowed a limited number of Afghan women to work for foreign agencies, but in July 2000 they issued an edict banning all women from such employment. It was hoped that the bakeries would be exempt, but in August 2000 the Taliban ordered their closure.

Poverty and bereavement were not the only scourges of war for Afghan women. Mujahideen soldiers fighting in Kabul in the early 1990s engaged in rape and sexual assault as a means of dishonoring entire communities and ensuring their surrender. RAWA says that throughout the years of war "women were looked upon as war booty, their bodies another battleground for belligerent parties."

The threat of violence kept many women on the run for years. Nooria used to live in Kabul with her husband and four children. "We had a good life. My husband was an engineer, an educated man," she said. They left in 1994. Civil war had torn up the city, she said; they didn't feel safe. They made for the northern town of Taloqan, where they had relatives, and started to establish a new home. But soon the Taliban came, and again they feared for their lives. Her husband was an ethnic Tajik, a natural supporter of the opposition Northern Alliance who had taken up arms against the Pashtun-dominated Taliban. "They didn't like us. They came to our house, beat down the door, threatened us, and took our property." Again they moved on, this time to a village further north, but that became a front line in fighting between the Taliban and the Northern Alliance. They sent her son to Iran to stay with

his uncle. The couple and their three daughters packed up their meager belongings and walked north again, ending up at the Khumkishlak refugee camp, a sad collection of tents and makeshift shelters on a dusty river plain near the border with Tajikistan. Nooria's husband died there in 2000. "He was weak, he didn't speak," she said, unable to explain how he died.

Nooria was left living the precarious existence of many women in Afghanistan, who, without a male breadwinner, are dependent on begging and charity. She lived with her daughters in a canvas tent with two mattresses, some blankets, and little else. They cooked on an open fire in front of the tent. A French aid agency provided them with basic food, but on Fridays she would sometimes go to the nearby town of Khoja Bahawuddin and wait in line with other burqa-clad women outside the mosque, hoping for a small handout as the men came out of midday prayers. A 10,000-afghani note was enough to buy one loaf of rough flat bread.

It was early November and the wind had started to blow up dust in icy, gritty gusts, signaling the start of winter. The U.S. bombing campaign against the Taliban was in full swing, and from Khumkishlak you could hear the thud of American bombs pounding Taliban front lines 20 miles across the plain. Nooria had no idea what the new war would bring. "We know what they are doing, we know they are fighting the Taliban, but all we think about is how we are going to eat," she said. "If peace comes, maybe we can go home, to Taloqan or Kabul. But we don't think about it. We only think about the day we are in."

A burqa-clad Afghan beggar sits outside a hospital in Quetta, Pakistan, November 1, 2001.

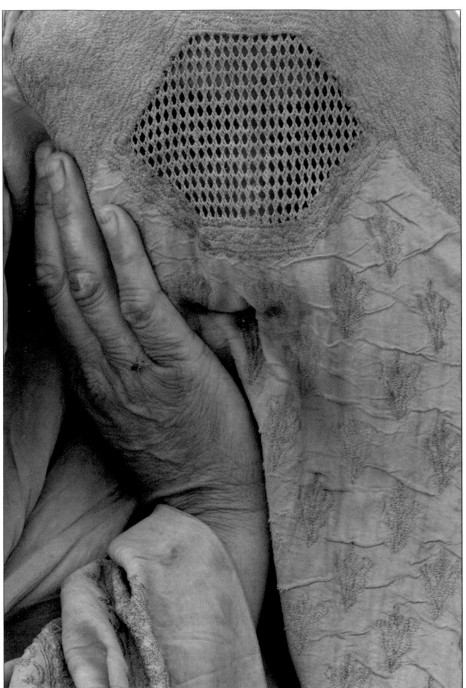

Adrees Latif

Gleb Garanich

Traditionally dressed Afghan women pass by two Northern Alliance tanks outside Taloqan, November 26, 2001.

Madina, an Afghan woman who is unsure of her own age, holds her son in their refugee home in a suburb of Kabul, December 8, 2001. Madina's daughter, Maqbula, aged four, was abducted and killed two years earlier and her eyes removed, according to her family and neighbors. Her death, and that of other children in Kabul, sparked rumors in the city that a gang was on the prowl kidnapping children for their organs. The rumors have not been confirmed.

Damir Sagolj

Yannis Behrakis

Afghan women shop for shoes in central Kabul, November 19, 2001.

An Afghan woman, with a mark on her hand allowing her to get humanitarian aid, pleads with a guard to let her receive food at a World Food Programme distribution point in Kabul's orphanage, December 10, 2001.

Damir Sagolj

An Afghan man rests in his cart as he waits for free food at a World Food Programme distribution point in Kabul, December 9, 2001.

Damir Sagolj

An Afghan woman holds a baby as she waits for humanitarian aid to be distributed in central Kabul, November 24, 2001.

Damir Sagolj

Damir Sagolj

A girl peers between poor Afghan women wearing burqas at a World Food Programme distribution point in the city of Kabul, December 10, 2001.

An elderly Afghan woman sits outside a line for humanitarian aid at a World Food Programme distribution point in Kabul's orphanage, December 10, 2001.

Damir Sagolj

An Afghan mother carries her daughter at a refugee camp near the Pakistan capital of Islamabad, November 8, 2001.

Jason Reed

Peter Andrews

Three Hazara girls sit in their cave in Bamiyan, December 15, 2001. The destruction of the giant Bamiyan Buddhas outraged world leaders, but a story of human horror also unfolded in the town and the surrounding area as forces of the Sunni Muslim Taliban, fired by a strict interpretation of Islam, forced tens of thousands of Shi'ite Muslims to flee into the mountains.

Afghan orphan girls show their painted hands on the first day of Eid al-Fitr in the Parvarishga orphanage in Kabul, December 16, 2001. Afghans marked the Muslim holiday of Eid al-Fitr for the first time without the Taliban after five years of their strict rule.

Damir Sagolj

Six-year-old Mozama leads the class in a lesson at the Rabia Beulkhi School for girls
in Queṭta's Hazaratown, November 2, 2001.

Adrees Latif

Andrees Latif

Jamilia, 13, reads over her English lesson in front of the class as her teacher
Madina stands by at the Rabia Beulkhi School for girls in Quetta's Hazaratown,
November 2, 2001. The 800-pupil school for Afghan refugee girls of all ages
teaches math, physics, English, history, and other subjects.

Yannis Behrakis

It was November 14, a day after the Taliban had fled Kabul. I was walking through the city in the early morning looking for signs of change. A group of about 100 women waited outside a bakery for food coupons. It was an extraordinary moment. I saw an unveiled face of a woman in a sea of burqas and shot a single frame. Then I put the camera down and stared at her. She had a mysterious smile; she looked back at me with a brave and resolute face. The morning sun seemed gently to stroke her cheek for the first time in five years. I was suddenly overcome by a feeling that I was witnessing colossal change. Her face sent back to me a wave of hope for the people of Afghanistan.

Yannis Behrakis

A young Afghan girl peeks
into the x-ray room of a
hospital for Afghan refugees
in Quetta, Pakistan,
November 1, 2001.

Adrees Latif

Damir Sagolj

Afghan women, with their burqas folded back showing their faces, look through the window of a bus in central Kabul, December 10, 2001. The U.N. World Food Programme carried out its biggest food distribution in the Afghan capital, handing out sacks of wheat to more than three-quarters of the war-ravaged city's population.

Afghans wait their turn to receive humanitarian aid at a World Food Programme
distribution point in Kabul, December 14, 2001.

Damir Sagolj

Peter Andrews

An Afghan woman has her hair styled at a beauty salon in Kabul, December 9, 2001. After the fall of the Taliban, Afghan women slowly returned to work and pursued more independent lives, although many still wore the head-to-toe burqas when outdoors.

An Afghan woman with chipped red
nail polish begs for money on a Kabul
street, November 21, 2001.

Yannis Behrakis

A Cautious Dawn

Paul Holmes

"Our country is nothing but a ruined land," Hamid Karzai declared at the inauguration of the new government. "Oh God, the journey is long, and I am a novice. I need your help."

The end came suddenly and under cover of darkness, but not with such haste that the Taliban had no time to plunder the national bank. On the night of November 12, as the Islamic militia and their al Qaeda allies retreated from Kabul, Haji Mullah Mohammad Ahmadi showed up at Bank Millie Afghan where he had been the Taliban's governor. Bearing the keys to the vault and escorted by a posse of gunmen, he calmly opened the locks, removed 5.3 million U.S. dollars and 22 million Pakistani rupees in cash, and then shut the vault again. Hours later, more armed Taliban returned to finish the job. They forced open the padlocks to a strongroom, loaded a mountain of local banknotes worth 18 billion afghanis onto pickup trucks, and sped off into the night down the road to Kandahar. "It is an act of national betrayal," declared Mahmoud Sharif, deputy head of the bank's strongroom section, his voice echoing through the dusty rooms that had been the repository of the country's meager financial reserves. "This money belonged to the people of Afghanistan."

The raid on the bank, a crumbling vestige of a forgotten age when the country was at peace, in many ways symbolized the sorry depths of Afghanistan's misery. The Taliban may have restored a measure of order to a lawless land during their harsh rule, but in the end they proved no different from the warlords, bandits, and smugglers who had laid the country to waste for their own power and enrichment following the end of the Soviet occupation in 1989. "You are here in the capital of Afghanistan in the Internet Age, but this is a country without proper electricity, a reliable water supply, food, or proper roads," lamented Mirza Gul Sagani, a political scientist at Kabul University, during my visit to his bare, chill office. He offered me tea, only to backtrack on his gesture of hospitality with profuse apologies after being told no wood was available to heat the water.

This, then, was Afghanistan's "Stunde Null," or Hour Zero, when, like Germany in 1945, a country devastated by war and traumatized by the ravages of a perverse ideology, emerged from the long darkness to confront the task of rebuilding a shattered nation. It was an uncertain awakening.

The Taliban, having captured Kabul virtually without a fight in 1996, were now gone, forced into flight by punishing U.S. air strikes and the lightning advance across the Shomali Plain north of the city by fighters from the Northern Alliance. Yet their entry into Kabul soon after dawn on November 13 with artificial flowers poking from the muzzles of their Kalashnikovs and triumphant smiles creasing their faces was greeted by the population as much with trepidation as with relief. The sounds of music, banned by the Taliban under their suffocating interpretation of Islamic Sharia law, swiftly returned to the streets, blaring from pocket transistors and car radios. Many men shaved off the long beards that the Taliban had made compulsory, unwound their turbans, and swapped their baggy Afghan trousers for denim jeans, a symbol of "Western decadence" that would have attracted a beating from the Taliban's enforcers. A few, but not many, women shed the confining, head-to-toe burqa veil. For four years from 1992 until the Taliban conquest of Kabul, factional warfare among the ethnic Tajik, Uzbek, Hazara, and other minorities that make up the Northern Alliance had reduced entire neighborhoods of the city to rubble and cost the lives of 50,000 civilians. Now, in defiance of international pressure to stay out of Kabul pending a post-Taliban political settlement, those same forces were back in control. Burhanuddin Rabbani, an ascetic professor of Islamic theology discredited by his rule over the chaos and fratricidal bloodshed during most of the period from 1992 to 1996, was again ensconced at the presidential palace.

Outside the capital, fighting continued as opposition Afghan forces on the ground and U.S. warplanes in the air pursued the relentless drive to force the Taliban from their two remaining strongholds, Kunduz in the north and Kandahar, the fundamentalist movement's spiritual birthplace, in the south.

Elsewhere, the very warlords whose bloody feuding and dizzying double-crosses bred the crime and insecurity that had assisted the Taliban's rise to power were back in the saddle, this time as partners in the American quest to capture Osama bin Laden and topple the Taliban for harboring him.

The western city of Herat, an ancient center of Afghan culture populated largely by Persian-speaking Tajiks and Shi'ite Muslims, was again the domain of the veteran Iranian-backed mujahideen commander Ismail Khan. In the north's largest city, Mazar-i-Sharif, former Communist General Abdul Rashid Dostum, an ethnic Uzbek, again ruled the roost. Reports by the International Committee of the Red Cross that 400 or more corpses littered the streets of the city following its capture on November 9 did nothing to diminish the fearsome reputation of Dostum's troops for brutality. In Jalalabad, in the east of the country near the border with Pakistan, a triumvirate of local warlords who had made the city a byword for corruption and a paradise for smugglers before the Taliban takeover carved up power again. In the Pashtun south, ragtag local armed militias forced off the roads by the Taliban returned to their checkpoints, robbing travelers and demanding tolls from truckers ferrying international relief supplies to a destitute population. "Under the Taliban we were safe," said one driver, who had been held up at gunpoint on the road to Kabul from Kandahar after the Taliban finally surrendered the ancient walled city in early December. "There was security. Now it's anarchy and getting steadily worse."

Of eight journalists killed covering Afghanistan in the weeks immediately following the start of U.S. air strikes on October 7, five fell victim to the reemerging lawlessness. One, Swedish television cameraman Ulf Stromberg, died when armed robbers shot through the door of a room where he was sleeping in a house he shared with other foreign reporters in the northern city of Taloqan. Four others—Australian cameraman Harry Burton and Afghan-born photographer Azizullah Haidari, both from Reuters;

Spaniard Julio Fuentes of *El Mundo* newspaper; and Italian Maria Grazia Cutuli of *Corriere della Sera*—were killed when six armed men ambushed their convoy on a stretch of dirt road near Sarobi, a small town east of Kabul, that had long been a hotbed of banditry during the lawless 1990s. Haidari, 33, had spent half his life as a refugee in Pakistan and had been returning to Kabul, the city of his birth, for the first time since 1983. Less than 48 hours into his homecoming, he was marched up a hill with his three colleagues and shot dead.

Into this growing anarchy stepped the international community with a plan to forge a broad-based government from among Afghanistan's myriad armed factions and ethnic groups and assist the country on a path to democracy. The speed of the Taliban's collapse had surprised even the United States, putting the political process out of sync with the military facts its bombing raids had created on the ground. The challenge was enormous. Afghanistan had not had a peaceful transition of power for decades. Those power-sharing deals that had been stitched together since 1992 among the components of the Northern Alliance, funded and armed by regional neighbors with interests of their own, rapidly fell apart into renewed factional fighting. This time, though, there was a sense that the mood and the stakes were different.

For one thing, a new generation of younger politicians had risen to prominence in the Northern Alliance as the political and military heirs of Ahmad Shah Masood, the famed mujahideen commander assassinated by Arab militants two days before September 11. Yunis Qanuni, Abdullah Abdullah, and Mohammad Fahim, all from Masood's Panjsher Valley heartland, were now calling the shots in the predominantly ethnic Tajik Jamiat-i-Islami party that forms the backbone of the Northern Alliance. They, not Rabbani, became the public face of the new order and, uncharacteristically for a land where power had stemmed from the barrel of a gun, they were insisting that it was not the Alliance's intention to monopolize power. For another, the international community was promising billions of dollars to support the recovery and reconstruction of a country bankrupt after 23 years of war and was brandishing that aid as a means of applying pressure. Two weeks after the Taliban fled Kabul, a delegation from the Northern Alliance led by Qanuni sat down to United Nations-sponsored talks at the secluded Petersberg hotel above the River Rhine outside Bonn, Germany, with representatives of three exiled groups, one loyal to former king Zahir Shah, another mainly Pashtun group backed by Pakistan, and a third supported by Iran. "You must not allow the mistakes of the past to be repeated, particularly those of 1992," U.N. Secretary-General Kofi Annan admonished the assembled rivals in a speech read at the opening session by his special envoy for Afghanistan, Lakhdar Brahimi. "To many skeptics it appears that is precisely that which you are about to do," Annan said. "You must prove them wrong."

The talks among the factions, many of whose delegates had not met since childhood in prewar Afghanistan, got off to an inauspicious start and swiftly hit snags over the carve-up of posts in a new interim administration. The most prominent Pashtun at the gathering, Haji Abdul Qadir, governor of the eastern province of Nangahar and the second-ranked member of the Northern Alliance delegation, walked out early on, complaining that the traditionally dominant ethnic group was not adequately represented. He came back after extracting the promise of a ministry. There were also grumblings back in Afghanistan, led by a bitter Rabbani, increasingly sidelined but still recognized by the United Nations as the country's nominal president. The white-bearded theologian's objections to the deal emerging in Bonn, expounded in rambling news conferences at the presidential palace, exposed deep divisions within the Northern Alliance between an old guard of leaders from the anti-Soviet war of the 1980s eager to retain power and the new generation of 40-somethings represented at the talks by Qanuni.

"We hope that Rabbani will understand the current situation and the sensitivity of issues and take the people's interests into account," a frustrated Qanuni declared as the talks dragged on. "This is a very golden opportunity which must be seized."

Seized it was, but only after almost nine days of exhausting haggling, heavy U.S. and U.N. pressure on a recalcitrant Rabbani, and arm twisting from foreign diplomats hovering in the wings at the Petersberg hotel. "The international community as a whole is standing in the background and glaring at the Afghans," said one Western envoy. "If they want to carry on as miserable squabbling people getting our aid and occasional bombing, that's their choice."

The accord signed early on December 5 created an interim government of 30 members to rule for six months until a Loya Jirga, or traditional grand assembly, could be held to appoint a broader transitional authority to take Afghanistan to unprecedented elections by mid-2004. It also provided for the deployment of a U.N.-mandated security force, though the details were left vague. December 22 was set as the date for the administration's installation. The Northern Alliance, with most of the country under its control, was awarded the three most powerful ministries, with Qanuni as interior minister, military chief Fahim as defense minister, and Abdullah Abdullah at foreign affairs. The man chosen to lead Afghanistan away from unremitting war, 43-year-old Pashtun tribal elder Hamid Karzai, had stayed away from the talks to negotiate the Taliban surrender of Kandahar. Tall and balding with a trim salt-and-pepper beard, he had been deputy foreign minister from 1992 to 1994 and spent much of the 1980s in the United States, where his family ran Afghan restaurants. A scion of a royalist family, he enjoyed strong Western support but was little known to Afghans outside his Popalzai tribal group.

Karzai's relative anonymity seemed to matter little on the streets of Kabul. There was a joke among journalists reporting from the capital that every question directed at any Afghan about their hopes for the future would be met with the answer "peace, stability, and a broad-based government." It was a joke that contained more than a seed of truth. Among dissenters in positions of evaporating power there were loud complaints that the new administration was unrepresentative and threats to put a spoke in its wheels. Rabbani, in a parting shot, railed ominously against yet more foreign interference in Afghanistan's affairs and bemoaned the humiliation of a generation of leaders of the anti-Soviet jihad "who struggled mountain by mountain, valley by valley against the aggressors." Dostum, from his northern bastion of Mazar-i-Sharif, threatened to boycott the new government and ban its ministers from his turf. Among ordinary Afghans, more than half of whom had known nothing but war and misery, there was little sympathy for such sour grapes. "We'll support anyone who serves the country and is for Afghanistan," said one Northern Alliance soldier,

Said U. Rahman, in a comment typical of the mood on the dusty streets of Kabul. "We don't care if he is a Pashtun, a Tajik, or anything else as long as he tries to restore peace and security."

The Afghans were literally sick and tired of the fighting. It showed in the drawn faces of stunted, malnourished children fed an unrelenting diet of flat nan bread and in the amputees maimed by land mines in one of the world's most heavily mined countries. Reliable statistics are hard to come by on Afghanistan. But after almost a quarter century of continuous war, the worst drought in three decades, and the ravages of the Taliban's ruinous attempt to take the country back 1,300 years to some imagined Islamic utopia, few would argue that it has some of the world's grimmest statistics. More than one-quarter of all children die before the age of five, and half of those that survive suffer from chronic malnutrition, according to U.N. estimates. Life expectancy hovers somewhere just above 40, and a man or woman in what the West would consider the prime of life can easily look 60 or 70. Only about 12 percent of Afghans have access to adequate sanitation. One-third of the population in a country that once exported produce is dependent on food aid.

Now, with the Taliban gone, international relief was again starting to flow into the country, hesitantly at first because of uncertain security and patchily because of remaining pockets of Taliban and al Qaeda resistance. When the World Food Programme began its first major handout of wheat in Kabul in early December, distribution points in the city were overwhelmed by surging crowds. Refugees who had fled fighting and drought to Iran and Pakistan were starting, albeit slowly and in modest numbers, to return to shattered homes to rebuild ruined lives. There were other signs too of a cautious new dawn.

Under the Taliban, it was an offense to watch television. Now satellite dishes fashioned from thin sheets of tin imported from Pakistan were sprouting from rooftops. "Since the Taliban left, all we've done is make satellite dishes," said Mohammad Khaled, a 22-year-old metalworker, who stopped making water pumps and turned to this lucrative new line almost as soon as the militia pulled out of Kabul. "It's better business than anything else," he declared, as the boys who worked for him beat triangular strips of tin printed with the words "Kountry Cookin' charcoal lighter fluid" into shape on the broken pavement outside his downtown workshop. Within a week of the Taliban retreat, Kabul Television came back on the air after a five-year blackout with a three-hour program of music, cartoons, interviews, and news. The broadcast was introduced by 16-year-old Mariam Shakebar. Aged 11 in 1996, she lost her job as a presenter of children's programs when the Taliban banned women from almost all work. "Greetings, viewers, we hope you are all well," declared Mariam's male and relatively clean shaven co-presenter Shamsuddin Hamid. "We're glad to have destroyed terrorism and the Taliban and to be able to present this program to you."

Cockfighting, prohibited by the Taliban, returned to the back streets of Kabul's teeming bazaars. Traffic police, one of the few national institutions to have functioned through all the carnage and chaos of the previous 23 years, found a new lease on life directing cars, taxis, carts, and the occasional flock of distinctive fat-tailed Afghan sheep along the capital's potholed roads. Mohammad Saleh was fired from the force by the Taliban along with 300 other traffic

policemen for alleged links with Communism. As soon as the Taliban rumbled out of town in their tanks, armored personnel carriers, and pickups, he shaved off his beard and donned his 22-year-old shabby brown serge uniform. "I was over the moon," the 40-year-old officer said during a break from directing the traffic at the Zambaq crossroads in central Kabul. "We're not getting a salary at the moment. We're just doing our duty and serving our country."

Women, banned from appearing in public without a male relative, were back on the streets unaccompanied, strolling in twos, threes, and fours, and foraging at the city's open-air produce stalls for whatever sustenance they could afford to buy. Almost all continued to wear their enveloping blue burqas, too distrustful of the country's de facto rulers or too steeped in Afghanistan's Islamic traditions to want to shed the veil. In a subtle shift of fashion, though, many women left the shorter front section open, revealing smart trousers and shoes in what would have rated as gross indecency just a few weeks earlier. Sports players, harshly restricted by the Taliban in how they could dress and compete, returned with enthusiasm to their neglected pursuits—to soccer stadiums that had been turned into public execution grounds by the Taliban, to weight-lifting gyms, where they quickly restored posters of admired bodybuilders like Sylvester Stallone to the walls, and to boxing and wrestling clubs. United Nations and other aid agencies, which had pulled out their international staff under the Taliban or after September 11, reopened offices in Kabul and other cities and again employed the women they had been forced by the Taliban to lay off. Men, for the first time in five years, were dancing with women again at weddings, and when Afghans celebrated the Eid al-Fitr holiday that marks the end of the Muslim fasting month of Ramadan, it was with celebratory gunfire, cakes, and music in an outpouring of merriment that had been anathema to the Taliban.

These were the superficial signs of a slow return to normality, to a way of life that for many were vague memories from the days of royal rule before 1979. For the majority of Afghans too young to have tasted peace, it was an inkling of what a world without fighting and fanaticism could resemble. Yet one did not have to dig deeply to see that this was a country facing a monumental battle to turn the tide of misery and deprivation.

It is a measure of Afghanistan's dire condition that the country scavenges through castoffs of a more affluent world to serve its basic needs. Steel 40-foot shipping containers are one of the most ubiquitous features of modern Afghanistan, put to use as simple dwellings, shops, storerooms, and—grimly—prisons for captured enemy fighters. Shoemaking, one of the few domestic cottage industries, relies on imported scrap rubber. Because of fighting or drought, fields and vineyards have lain untended for years. Few adults are gainfully employed in a country where children are often the only breadwinners.

Arshad, 12, and his four brothers aged six to 14 toil 11 hours a day in their spartan mud-brick home in northern Kabul, weaving brightly patterned kilim rugs to bring in 20 dollars a month to support a family of 11. "This is the only way we have to earn a living," said the boys' father, Sayed Fahim, 40, who lost a leg fighting for the communist-backed army 20 years ago. "If they didn't work, we'd starve."

Girls were barred from formal schooling by the Taliban, but the damage to an already primitive education system ran far deeper. The majority of teachers were women and thus unable to work, meaning that boys, too, were deprived of an education. Schools are starting up again, but without books, basic teaching equipment, or the money to pay teachers a salary.

"In 1978 we had 189 schools in our region. Under Taliban rule only seven of these managed to keep going," said Mahmoud Daoud Barak, the new director of education in Kandahar, where some 90 schools have begun to function with 120,000 pupils, some of them young adults trying to make up for the lost years of learning. "We need to double the number of schools and students we have now just to reach the point where we were 24 years ago," Barak said.

The health system, where women were a mainstay in the provision of basic care, is in tatters, and mental health experts are only just beginning to understand the depth of the psychological trauma the conflict has inflicted. "Almost all our people have some psychological problems, but especially our children," said Abdul Mannan Haqyar, head of the Kabul Mental Health Hospital. "When children witness a traumatic event like a rocket or bomb attack, their minds can become obsessed with that incident," he said. "They feel human life has no value."

So deep is the destitution of Afghanistan that when the interim government's ministers, many of them back in the country for the first time since the Soviet occupation, took up their posts, the only equipment they had to work with were basic office-supply start-up kits provided by the United Nations. Staff in public service had not been paid for months. Early estimates were that the new government would need $100 million immediately just to pay the back salaries and cover the wages bill for its six months in office.

Estimates of how much international aid would be needed over 10 years to rebuild the country ranged from $15 billion to $22 billion.

"This is a government that has literally empty coffers," said Mark Malloch-Brown, head of the United Nations Development Programme tasked with coordinating the flow of funds. "The central bank vaults are an echo chamber."

The enormity of the challenge and the urgency were evident on December 22 at the inauguration of Afghanistan's new government in a chill meeting hall of the Interior Ministry in Kabul. The time had come to start fashioning a central authority for a country splintered into private fiefdoms and to generate a common identity in a land that for so long had known only hatred and division. Outside the gathering, British Royal Marine commandos, the vanguard of a multinational security force in the making, stood guard with Northern Alliance soldiers and Afghan security forces, whose freshly painted white helmets identified them as members of a nascent police force.

Inside the chamber, beneath a giant portrait of Ahmad Shah Masood, Karzai shared the podium with many of the warlords who had brought the country to its knees. Rabbani, seemingly resigned to his departure from the scene, exchanged an embrace with the man on whose shoulders the burden of healing Afghanistan's wounds would now fall. Two thousand guests sat in the audience at a gathering that brought together former foes and long-time friends, elders in turbans, and diplomats from countries reopening missions after a decade of neglect of Afghanistan's plight.

Women, struggling to regain the active role in Afghan life that the long years of fighting and the rule of the Taliban had denied them, were segregated from the men but none wore the burqa. Near them sat General Tommy Franks, commander of the U.S.-led war that had chased the Taliban from power. No mention was made in the speeches that echoed through the hall on a crackling sound system of the American part in the shaping of these events, a reflection perhaps of the sensitivities forged over centuries of foreign invasion to outside involvement in Afghanistan's troubled destiny.

Much, though, was made by Karzai of the need finally for unity in a land where tribal and ethnic enmities and even the sheer geography of towering mountains and harsh desert had conspired to deny its people the fruits of peace and the promise of the modern world beyond their borders. Cloaked in a flowing green- and purple-striped traditional Uzbek robe and speaking in both Pashto and Dari, the two main languages of Afghanistan, he seemed to embody that hope as he outlined a 13-point plan to turn the tide of despair.

A sense of history pervaded the ceremony, opened and closed with readings from the Koran. But there was also a sense of awe at the magnitude of the task that lay ahead.

"Our country is nothing but a ruined land," Karzai declared. "Oh God, the journey is long, and I am a novice. I need your help."

Sayed Salahuddin

Having been forbidden for five years under Taliban rule to cut his beard, regaining the freedom to do so was a joyful event for this young man. He didn't hesitate. The dust from the fleeing zealots' sandals had barely settled when he entered this Kabul barbershop for a shave. There was no long line, perhaps because people were still nervous. But nothing was going to stop him. "I want to get rid of it because I was forced to grow it against my will," he said. "Now I am free, and I want to exercise my own free will."

I felt strongly that morning that freedom was not only a matter of choice but a right for all men and women. I hoped that Afghanistan would never again see rulers who used religion for their own ends and under a double standard— saying that the aim was democracy or freedom.

Looking at the man being shaved, I couldn't rid myself of a nagging doubt. The Taliban had forced men to grow their beards, checking their length against that of a man's fist. Would their successors, the Northern Alliance, veer to the other extreme? In the immediate aftermath of the ousting of the Taliban, they looked askance at men who didn't cut their beards. Such men, some even insinuated, favored the Taliban. Where was the freedom in that?

I prayed that this young Afghan man, who had raced with such delight to shave his beard, and others like him, would forever enjoy the freedom to choose for themselves.

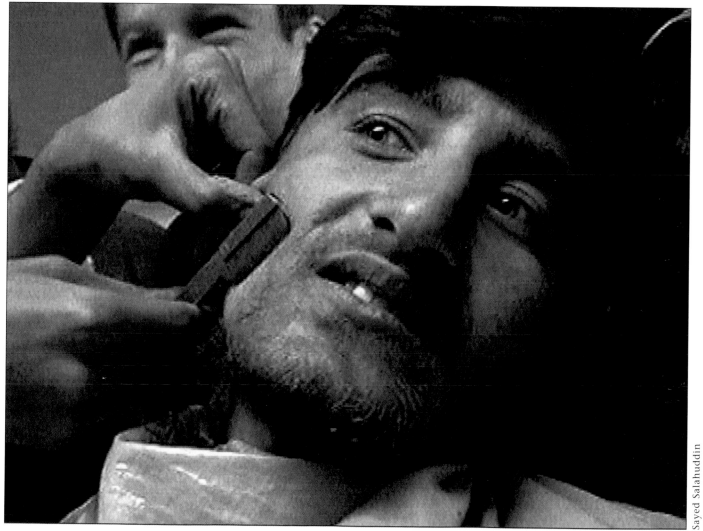

Sayed Salahuddin

Children peer through the window of a barber shop in Kabul while an Afghan man
has his long beard shaved for the first time after five years of Taliban rule ended,
November 20, 2001.

Damir Sagolj

Afghan men enjoy a hot bath at a Haman (bathhouse) in the Moradhani neighborhood of Kabul, November 18, 2001. Under its strict interpretation of Islam, the Taliban banned music, ordered all adult men to wear a beard long enough to be clutched in a fist, and forbade women, hidden behind head-to-toe burqas, to work or study. Bathhouses were also banned.

Yannis Behrakis

Men fight to enter the Bakhtar cinema in central Kabul to see the first public film shown since the fall of the Taliban, November 19, 2001. Scuffles broke out in front of the cinema as the men fought their way in to see the Afghan movie "Urur" or "Ascension." Military police beat back the crowd and restored order among excited film-goers desperate to get into the 600-seat cinema.

Yannis Behrakis

Yannis Behrakis

An Afghan cinema technician operates a movie projector in the Bakhtar cinema in central Kabul at the first public film show since the fall of the Taliban, November 19, 2001.

Afghan boys are seen through a slot in a door as they sit on the floor of a home-based school in Kabul, December 2, 2001. The school, operating secretly for a year under the strict Taliban regime, has now opened its doors for all children ready to pay a small monthly fee.

Damir Sagolj

Afghan men sell pictures of women, strictly prohibited during Taliban rule, from their small shop in central Kabul, December 6, 2001.

Damir Sagolj

An Afghan girl reads from the board in a home-based school in Kabul,
December 2, 2001.

Damir Sagolj

A burqa-clad woman tries a Western dress in Kabul, December 27, 2001. After five years of Taliban rule, when the burqa shrouded women from head to toe and tailors were not allowed to measure female clients, Kabul's fashion industry has been reborn.

Erik de Castro

A soldier sits with his rifle guarding the entrance to Afghanistan's national museum in Kabul, December 1, 2001. A pile of masonry in a dusty storeroom of the museum was all that was left of several ancient statues. Two millennia old, they were hacked to pieces by the Taliban's religious police in just two days.

Damir Sagolj

Damir Sagolj

Afghan men load worthless afghani notes in bags in an underground strongroom of the country's national bank in Kabul, November 29, 2001. Fleeing Taliban members plundered Afghanistan's national bank and made off with millions of dollars in cash during their hurried retreat from Kabul. Only bundles of worthless 100- and 500-afghani notes, stacked in dusty piles on the ground, were left behind.

Afghan actors perform in a stage play at a damaged theater in Kabul, January 2, 2002. Drama was banned during Taliban rule.

Erik de Castro

Marines carry the Stars and Stripes during a ceremony at the American embassy in Kabul, December 17, 2001. The United States reestablished a diplomatic presence in the Afghan capital for the first time since its diplomats left the city shortly before the end of the Soviet occupation in 1989. On a cold and drizzly afternoon, two Marines hoisted the same Stars and Stripes on the same flagpole from which it was taken down on January 30, 1989.

Damir Sagolj

A Marine stands guard outside the entrance to the American Embassy in Kabul, December 18, 2001. The Stars and Stripes flew over the U.S. Embassy in Kabul for the first time in almost 12 years, as the United States reopened its mission in time for the installation of a new Afghan government.

Peter Andrews

British Royal Marine commandos exit a C-130 plane at Bagram Air Base in Afghanistan, December 20, 2001. The Marines, flown in from the Middle East, were the lead element of a multinational security force being deployed in Kabul.

Peter Andrews

Leader of the new interim government Hamid Karzai (right) presents Burhanuddin
Rabbani (left), former President of Afghanistan, with an academic certificate awarded
to him by the academy of sciences following the swearing-in ceremony at the
Interior Ministry building in Kabul, December 22, 2001. A soft-spoken Afghan
aristocrat, Karzai formally took up the reins of power as head of a U.N.-backed
interim government.

Peter Andrews

Hamid Karzai listens to a speech by
Burhanuddin Rabbani, former President
of Afghanistan, after being sworn in as
leader of an interim government in
Kabul, December 22, 2001.

Peter Andrews

Hamid Karzai (third right—front), his cabinet members, and dignitaries stand as the national anthem of Afghanistan is played at the inauguration of the new interim government in Kabul, December 22, 2001. In the background is a giant poster of Ahmad Shah Masood, a formidable military tactician and commander who was assassinated in early September.

Peter Andrews

Mariam Shakebar, a 16-year-old Afghan girl, welcomes back Kabul television viewers after a five-year blackout ordered by the Taliban, November 18, 2001.

Shamil Zhumatov

An Afghan woman wearing a burqa watches television in an electronics shop on Nadir Pashtun street in Kabul, November 19, 2001.

Shamil Zhumatov

Afghans sing and play music in their home on the first day of Eid al-Fitr, in Kabul, December 16, 2001. Afghans marked the Muslim holiday of Eid al-Fitr for the first time without the Taliban, who banned music.

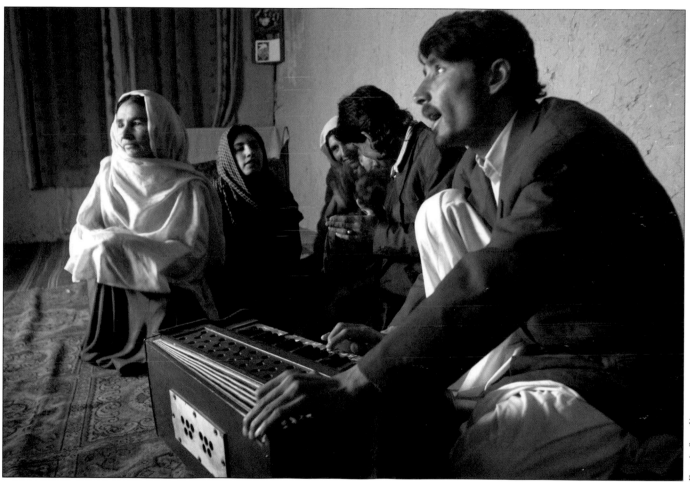

Damir Sagolj

A boxer exercises under the poster of the legendary American champion Muhammad Ali at a boxing club in the suburbs of Kabul, November 24, 2001. Under strict Taliban rule, boxing was forbidden as "anti-Islamic" and clubs could operate only behind closed doors.

Damir Sagolj

Nickwalli, a 12-year-old Afghan boy who was wounded after he touched and set off an unexploded U.S. cluster bomb dropped during the raids on Kabul, lies on a hospital bed, November 22, 2001. The United States came under criticism from human-rights groups for using cluster bombs.

Damir Sagolj

Doctor Sanjay Shivpuri from India works at the children's hospital in Kabul, November 24, 2001. A team of doctors from the Indian army operated at the hospital named after former Indian Prime Minister Indira Gandhi.

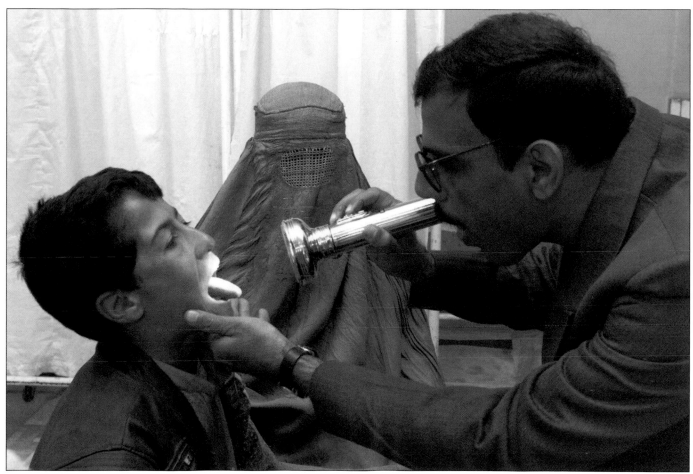

Shamil Zhumatov

Afghan men attend a cockfight in a back
street of Kabul's bazaar, November 30,
2001. Cockfighting, a sport popular
with gamblers, was forbidden during the
years of strict Taliban rule.

Damir Sagolj

An Afghan boy flies a kite, forbidden
during Taliban rule, from a roof in
central Kabul, December 7, 2001.

Damir Sagolj

Journalists and Photojournalists

Peter Andrews

Peter Andrews was born in Kano, Nigeria, in 1961, grew up in Poland from 1966, and emigrated to Canada in 1980. In 1984, having studied at Ottawa University, he became a photographer. He returned to Europe in 1989 to work for AP, and in 1991 he joined Reuters during the first coup in Moscow. In 1996 he moved to Johannesburg as Chief Photographer for Southern Africa, and in 1999 he became Chief Photographer for Eastern and Southern Africa in Nairobi.

Yannis Behrakis

Yannis Behrakis was born in Athens in 1960 and has worked for Reuters since 1987. He has covered wars in the former Yugoslavia and in Chechnya as well as stories in Asia, Africa, the Middle East, and Eastern Europe and events at the last three Olympic Games. He has won numerous photo awards. In 2000 the President of the Greek Republic presented him with the highest Greek journalism award of the Botsis foundation.

Erik de Castro

Erik de Castro was born in the Philippines in 1960. He started his career in photojournalism in 1980 in Baguio City in the northern Philippines, working at a small community newspaper called *The Gold Ore*. He joined United Press International in 1983 and Reuters in 1985. Since then he has been based in the Philippines.

Mikhail Evstafiev

Mikhail Evstafiev graduated from the Moscow State University with a master's degree in journalism. In 1986 he volunteered to serve with the Soviet military in Afghanistan, where he spent two years. In 1990 he switched from reporting to photography and covered the collapse of the Soviet Union and the wars in Chechnya and Bosnia. Since 1996 he has worked for Reuters as a photographer/editor, based in Moscow, London, and Washington, D.C. He has written a book, *Two Steps from Heaven*, about the Soviet war in Afghanistan.

David Fox

David Fox was born in England in 1962 but raised in Africa, where he started work on the *Rhodesian Herald* in 1979. He joined Reuters full-time in 1991 and has covered conflicts and natural disasters in Africa, Asia, the Middle East, and Europe. He was Bureau Chief in East Africa during one of the most turbulent times in its history, from 1998 to 2000, reporting on war in Somalia, Ethiopia, Eritrea, Sudan, Rwanda, Burundi, and Zaire.

Gleb Garanich

Gleb Garanich was born on Sakhalin Island, Russia, in 1969. He studied in Ukraine at the Kharkov Aviation Institute. His career in photography began in 1990 at a national news agency. In 1995 he joined Reuters. He has covered many major news stories, including the 1991 and 1993 coup attempts in Moscow and conflicts in Nagorno-Karabakh and Chechnya.

Tom Heneghan

Tom Heneghan first visited Afghanistan in 1976. Ten years later, he returned as Reuters first reporter there since the 1979 Soviet invasion. After September 11, he followed the Afghan crisis from Peshawar, covered transition talks in Bonn, and reported from post-Taliban Kabul. Born in New York in 1951, Heneghan joined Reuters in 1977 and has worked in London, Vienna, Geneva, Islamabad, Bangkok, Hong Kong, Bonn, and Paris, where he is now chief political correspondent for France.

Jim Hollander

Jim Hollander was born in 1949 in the United States. He began his career as a photojournalist in the mid-1970s. In 1980 he joined UPI. After the war in Lebanon in 1982, he was transferred to Tel Aviv as UPI Chief Photographer, and in 1985 he joined Reuters. He became Chief Photographer, Israel and covered many key developments there.

Paul Holmes

Born in 1955 in London, Paul Holmes began working as a journalist in Germany in 1979 and joined Reuters in London in 1982. His postings have taken him to London, Bonn, Rome, Vienna, Jerusalem, and Paris with short-term assignments around the world. He has covered conflicts in the Balkans, Somalia, and the Caucasus and was the only Reuters correspondent to cover the 1991 Gulf War from both sides. After September 11, he reported from both New York and Kabul.

Pawel Kopczynski

Pawel Kopczynski was born in 1971 in Warsaw, Poland. He graduated from Photo-technical College with a diploma in news photography. He began working as a news photographer in 1987, first for daily newspapers, then for the Polish Press Agency, and finally for Reuters, which he joined in 1995. Kopczynski has covered a wide variety of major world events, including the war in the former Yugoslavia, the Kosovo refugee crisis, the Soccer World Cup, the Winter Olympics, and the rising of tensions between India and Pakistan.

Jerry Lampen

Jerry Lampen was born in Rotterdam in 1961. He began his career in photography in November 1981 at a local Rotterdam agency, covering news events and sports. In August 1985 he got a staff job at United Photos in Haarlem, the Netherlands. Lampen left the agency in December 1997 to return to Rotterdam, where he worked with two picture agencies and started his career with Reuters, covering sports and general news.

Adrees Latif

Adrees Latif was born in 1973 in Lahore, Pakistan. He studied journalism at the University of Houston. Major stories he covered for Reuters include the 2000 Sydney Olympics, the Haj pilgrimage to Mecca in Saudi Arabia, and the Pakistan-India crisis. He is currently based in Los Angeles, California.

David Loh

Penang-born David S.T. Loh, 34, has worked as a professional photographer for the past 11 years. He has been a staff photographer at Reuters since 1995 and is now based in Singapore as photographer/pictures subeditor, Reuters Asia.

Jane Macartney

Jane Macartney was born and grew up in Borneo and read Chinese at Durham University. After three years working for UPI in China, she joined Reuters in Hong Kong and became bureau chief in Islamabad in 1992, arriving just three days before the mujahideen turned their guns on each other. She was bureau chief in Beijing from 1994 to the end of 1997 and became news editor in Tokyo in 2000. Macartney arrived in Islamabad on September 14, 2001, to coordinate Reuters coverage of the war in Afghanistan.

Andrew Marshall

Andrew Marshall has been a Reuters journalist for eight years and has covered a number of hot spots including Northern Ireland, East Timor, and Afghanistan. A graduate in English and economics from Cambridge University, he began his journalism career as a Reuters graduate trainee in 1994. He is now Deputy Bureau Chief in Bangkok, Thailand. Marshall was born in Edinburgh, Scotland, in 1971.

Dylan Martinez

Dylan Martinez was born in Barcelona to Argentine parents in 1969 and moved to Britain a year later. He began taking pictures for music magazines and record companies and then moved onto Sygma and the *Sunday Mirror*. He started to freelance for Reuters in 1991 and was made staff photographer in 1994. He worked in Asia, based in Vietnam, from 1996 to 1998 and is now based in Rome.

David Mercado

David Mercado, 44, was born in Cochabamba, Bolivia. He toured parts of Europe and recorded five albums as a musician playing Andean folk music before becoming a photographer. His photographic career began in 1989 with *Epoca* magazine in La Paz, followed by extensive work with the prominent newspaper *La Razon* and then with the national photo agency, Jatha Fotos. Mercado began working occasionally for Reuters in 1995 and then full-time in 1997.

Jeff Mitchell

Jeff Mitchell worked as a Staff Photographer at the *Arkansas Gazette* from 1980 to 1988 and then as Director of Photography until the paper closed in 1991. He became associated with Reuters News Pictures in 1992, anchoring the Clinton Presidential Campaign coverage in Little Rock, Arkansas. He relocated to Dallas, Texas, in 1999.

Bobby (Romeo) Ranoco

Bobby Ranoco, 43, started his career in photojournalism at UPI in Manila. He moved to Reuters in 1984 on the invitation of his uncle, the late Reuters photographer Willie Vicoy. In 1986 Vicoy was killed by New People's Army rebels in the ambush of a military convoy in Cagayan valley, and Ranoco took over his post. He has become one of Reuters Philippines' most seasoned news photographers.

Jason Reed

Jason Reed was born in Sydney in 1970 and joined Reuters during his first year in college. In 1994 he moved to Hong Kong, where in 1997 he covered the handover of the British colony to Chinese rule. He moved with Reuters to Singapore, then to Thailand, assuming additional responsibility for picture coverage in Myanmar, Laos, and Cambodia. On several occasions Reed has worked in Pakistan and Afghanistan.

Rosalind Russell

Rosalind Russell was born in Manchester, England, in 1969. She studied at University College London and joined Reuters in 1996. Russell was posted to Nairobi in 1998 and covered wars in Ethiopia, Eritrea, and Congo and famine in Sudan and Somalia. Since 2001 she has been based in Tbilisi, Georgia. She spent a month in Afghanistan in November 2001, trekking on horseback to the front line north of Kabul. Hours after the Taliban fled, Russell entered the capital with the Northern Alliance.

Damir Sagolj

Damir Sagolj was born in Sarajevo in 1971. He worked with the Paris-based Sipa press agency for several years before joining Reuters in 1996 as Bosnian photographer.

Sayed Salahuddin

Born in 1971 in Kabul, Sayed Salahuddin studied at Kabul University. After working for the *Kabul Times*, he joined the BBC as a translator. He moved to Reuters in mid-1996, just in time to cover the arrival of the Taliban. In the U.S.-led war on Afghanistan, Salahuddin stayed in Kabul, providing text, pictures, and television coverage of the campaign. He was the first to get out news of the arrival of the Northern Alliance.

Syed Haider Shah

Syed Haider Shah was born in Peshawar, Pakistan, in 1956. He started working as a photojournalist for national dailies from 1974, also working as a freelancer for Reuters. He was one of the few photographers who accompanied the Afghan mujahideen inside Afghanistan during and after the Soviet invasion in 1979, and his photos were published around the world.

Jorge Silva

Mexican Jorge Silva, 26, has been a freelancer for Reuters in Guatemala since April 2000. Silva joined Reuters from AFP and had previously worked with the local Mexican agency Cuartoscuro. He has a degree in Communications Studies from the UNAM (Autonomous University of Mexico).

Brian Williams

Brian Williams is an Australian who joined Reuters in 1969 from the *Melbourne Age*. After working in New York, he covered the wars in Vietnam and Cambodia and later opened a bureau in Sydney. He was based in Islamabad to report the Afghan-Soviet war. He was in New Delhi from 1983–1987 and then became media news editor for the Americas, before working in Asia as chief correspondent for Japan and North Korea. He became chief correspondent for Britain and Ireland in 1999.

Shamil Zhumatov

Shamil Zhumatov was born in Almaty, Kazakhstan, in 1971. He studied journalism at Kazakh State University and from 1987 worked as a photographer for the Kazakhstan newspaper *Leninskaya Smena*. He left in 1990 to work as a photographer for the Kazakh State Information Agency (the TASS department in Kazakhstan). Since 1994 he has been with Reuters, covering Kazakhstan, Kyrgyzstan, Tajikistan, Turkmenistan, and Uzbekistan.

Additional pictures by **Patrick de Noirmont** and **Muzammil Pasha**.